Stanley Lover's

Masterclass

For Soccer Officials

FROM *REFEREE*
MAGAZINE AND THE
NATIONAL ASSOCIATION
OF SPORTS OFFICIALS

Stanley Lover's Masterclass for Soccer Officials

Copyright © 2003 by Stanley Lover.

Cover design by Rob VanKammen, Graphic Designer, *Referee* Magazine

ISBN 1-58208-030-5

Printed in the United States of America.

Table of Contents

Introduction

Skating on ice is very difficult, at least it is for me. My rare attempts to stay upright, on bits of metal with minds of their own, always end the same way — a thumping fall with legs splayed high and a bruised rear end. Watching the World Ice Skating Championship, held in Washington in 2003, I envied the ease and confidence of the young people performing programs of balletic poetry with such athletic grace. I wondered how many thousands of hours they had devoted to attain that level.

I observed something else, something that marks the difference between an average and an outstanding performance in the art of creating beauty in sport. The difference was the degree of passion, belief and dedication, expressed by each contestant.

All were exceptional, but those who emerged as champions displayed an extra depth of passion. No anxious frowns, not a flicker of doubt, just self-assured smiles and natural flowing movements from the first second to the final triumphant pose.

Sometimes it's like that in soccer. Often it appears among the most innocent of players, children chasing a ball. All smiles and giggles, they have the passion, the real feel for the fun of the sport. At a more senior level, natural ability to play is refined by those early fires of passion, feel and sheer joy of taking part.

It's like that, too, in soccer officials. You can tell who has the feel for the game, who wants it played to the spirit as well as the letter of the rules.

The purpose of this book is to help make the most of your passion for soccer, to inform, advise, broaden horizons, stimulate search for knowledge — all to refine your practical performance on the field.

Some readers will note that early chapters are based on parts of *Soccer Match Control,* written 30 years ago, and subsequently developed into a series of articles published in *Referee* magazine since 1997.

In the bibliography you will find selected publications recommended for study by all soccer officials. When you have absorbed the collective wisdom therein you will go into each match with the confidence and ease of those champion skaters, expressing your own depth of passion to keep soccer a clean, exciting, fun sport.

— Stanley Lover

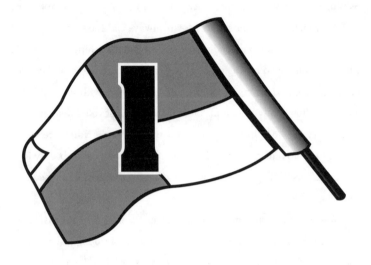

Magic
Kingdom
of Soccer

We had stopped for petrol. It was hot. The west African sun blazed into the tiny car and I felt uncomfortable from the remains of a fever that had left me weak after a hurried vaccination had gone wrong. Kurt, my companion, was busy with the attendant discussing quantity and price at the sole, sad-looking pump that must have been the original model designed when petrol was discovered. It looked as I felt — sick. It was in need of a rest, a coat of paint, elbow grease on parts meant to be bright and cheerful but now covered with grime and brick-red dust from the bush road. My mouth was dry, my body beginning to burn from the heat and the fever. Thin cotton shirt, white tropical shorts and open sandals were all that I wore, but I perspired.

We had only just started our journey on the road from Accra, the Ghana captial, to the Volta Dam. It was supposed to be the cool of the morning. The worst was yet to come. Could I last the whole day? Could I now suggest that we postpone the visit? Would Kurt agree to take me back to my bungalow, where I had a stock of cold drinks and a large fan that swished lazily, but efficiently and coolly, over my bed? I could rest there all day and be fit for the journey tomorrow. But no, it would cause too many complications.

I left the car and walked toward the nearest available shade by the wall of a small, one-story building that served as the house, office and storeroom of the petrol station attendant. He was now talking animatedly to Kurt, his wide hat flopping up and down rhythmically with the movement of his head as he made his point.

Approaching the house, I became aware of noise and movement on the balcony that jutted out over the entrance. What

I saw attracted my interest. Two small boys, no more than seven or eight years old, moved excitedly and happily on an area about three meters long by two meters wide. They were playing soccer. They were not aware of my presence as I watched. They were in a world of their own.

Poorly clothed, with thin bodies, their faces however carried constant broad smiles and displayed gleaming white teeth when their wide mouths broke into laughter.

They wriggled and jumped, kicked and pushed with the wild excitement of free expression. One boy picked up the ball by gripping his toes on a stray end of rag.

Apart from their restricted pitch the only accessory was a ball — a tight bundle of rags. No goalposts, corner flags, referee or assistants, but in their imagination they played out the most important match in the world. They wriggled and jumped, kicked and pushed with the wild excitement of free expression. One boy picked up the ball by gripping his toes on a stray end of rag. That caused both to burst into great shrieks of laughter and giggles. It was a joy to watch. I was transported into another world for what seemed an age, and yet it proved to be only a few minutes.

In their world they were the great Pele or another soccer idol, bobbing, weaving, beating formidable opponents with a body swerve, a drag-back, swift acceleration and scoring the winning goal in the World Cup Final with a brilliantly judged volley that crashed into the back of the net. In reality the rag ball came spinning down and landed in a puff of red dust at my feet. Two excited faces looked down, silently imploring me to throw back their ball. I did. The ball had hardly touched the balcony before a new World Cup Final began amid shouts, laughs and giggles in complete isolation from that other world of reality.

Those few moments gave me great joy and elation. My cares were forgotten. "Are you coming?" cried Kurt. I returned to the car feeling refreshed after that invigorating journey into another world: the magic kingdom of soccer, where a child with a ball is king.

Soccer and You

The sheer joy of watching those two boys playing their hearts out with a rag-tag ball made me realize what the game meant to me.

I relived my childhood years at play with anything at hand serving as a ball — a tight bundle of rags, cartons, any object I could move with foot, head or chest to put life into an inanimate object and test my skills. Graduating to a real ball (an old, fluffy tennis ball) was a great leap forward. What fun we had!

You need to know what soccer means to you because the value of what follows depends on your feelings about the game. Reflect on aspects of soccer that attracted you to become an official. Understanding your motivations will prepare you for the duties and responsibilities needed to safeguard the best interests of the game.

What is football, the rest of the world's term for soccer? What virtues made the game the most popular sport in the world? Dictionary definitions such as, "football … large, round, inflated ball; a game played with it," are not helpful in pointing the way toward the magnetism of the game.

Many enthusiasts are attracted by the pleasures of healthy exercise. An interesting description of that aspect of soccer was written by Richard Mulcaster, headmaster of Merchant Taylors' and St. Paul's schools in 1581:

"Football strengtheneth and brawneth the whole body and by provoking superfluities downward, it dischargeth the head and upper parts. It is good for the bowels and to drive down the stone and gravell from both the bladder and the kidneys.

"It helpeth weak hammes, by much moving, beginning at the meane and simple shankes by thickening of the fleshe no less than

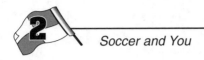

riding doth. Yet rash running and too much force oftentime breaketh some inward conduit and brineth ruptures."

There is truth in those observations, but hardly enough to explain the universal acceptance of soccer. Views on the game vary from this somewhat basic description to an all-embracing philosophical concept that introduces moral values and higher human qualities.

One of the game's attractions is its simplicity. It is an emotional experience. It has an unspoken universal language and the power to concentrate the attention of a large portion of the world's population

What is football, the rest of the world's term for soccer? What virtues made the game the most popular sport in the world?

on a peaceful pastime. People of all ages, sexes and nationalities have discovered the sport provides an exciting and yet relaxing therapy for life's daily problems. It could be argued with some justification that it is more widely practiced and discussed than love, the basic emotion of life. Every emotion, with its full range of expression, emerges during the uncertain ebb and flow of a contest between two great teams, engaged in a sporting battle, struggling for supremacy. The simple game of soccer is a means of expressing a range of emotions which few other activities can touch.

Perhaps you are attracted by the skills of individuals and experience moments of tingling excitement as masters of the game perform magical feats of control over body and ball or at the breathtaking power of a swift shot. Masters like Pele, Charlton, Zidane, Maradona, Beckham and Renaldo evoke those moments. Such players and many more are legendary figures in soccer folklore and will stir nostalgia for many years. Soccer legends are better known than many politicians who successfully fashioned great economies or generals who led great armies.

Passions for soccer often begin at an early age and last a lifetime. It's easy to understand how children will catch soccer fever if they live in the hotbed environment of a soccer-crazy household or in a locality sporting a famous team. Perhaps that was your particular nursery.

Soccer fever is not always caught at an early age, as seen in the remarkable growth of the game in North America. Many American adults, recently converted, have not experienced the childhood pleasures just described, but have been attracted to the game by the fire of enthusiasm in the eyes of youngsters scrimmaging with a soccer ball. The success of U.S. women's teams in world tournaments has drawn many females into the game — as players, referees and spectators. Those newcomers to the sport will ensure its solid continuation for they are the parents of current and future generations of soccer players.

It is a sobering thought that more people watched the 1974 World Cup series in Germany than watched the first manned moon landing. On reflection, that may not be so surprising because one is real and tangible, the other remote and bordering on the realms of fantasy.

Simple as the game is, soccer has its own subtle ingredients of mystery, suspense, drama and pathos, special qualities of spontaneous humor that bring life and brightness to many a dull heart. Is that what soccer means to you? Or are you attracted by its color, speed, athletic grace and power? Whatever your motives for being involved in the game, whether as player, coach, administrator or referee, there is no doubt your actions on and off the field will truthfully reflect your inner feelings for the sport.

Deciding to accept the role of arbitrator is to declare your personal commitment to the game. You have seen such a role is

neither popular nor glamorous, but it is respected by those who share your concern that the principles and reputation of the sport must be preserved. You will be joining, or have already joined, a small band of individuals prepared to withstand criticism and apply unselfish devotion to ensure the pleasures of the game are available for those who seek them. Your success in achieving that objective will be your reward. New match officials should know the task ahead will be difficult. Dedication will be tested on many occasions and in many ways.

Demands on match officials are more pressing as the competitive element has intensified. Skills, methods of play and tactics are more sophisticated. Courage, integrity, determination and more are needed in the current era of officials. Referees must be knowledgeable about game aspects that have hitherto been of only passing interest. Deeper awareness of physical and psychological factors, development of techniques in reading situations, knowledge of latest tactical innovations, constant reappraisal of fundamental principles and personal analysis are but some areas for study. Expert knowledge of the written laws doesn't equal match control.

Subsequent chapters in this book will look at facets of soccer covering tradition, history, technical and practical subjects. Here, I've tried to help you crystallize your understanding and inner feelings about the game. You will find pieces of the jigsaw that, when brought together at the end, will present a clear picture and point the way to the successful planning of your referee career.

Are there such people as typical referees? If there are, what qualities distinguish them from others? Top referees hold occupations such as factory managers, teachers and lecturers, engineers, salesmen, tradesmen, company directors, civil servants, and accountants. All involve some degree of formal training, personal application and responsibility. Nearly all require good relationships with other people whether in a business or educational capacity.

Communicating successfully with others is an important career requirement. Experience of life, maturity and integrity are essential to most successful careers. From my observation, referees at that level show a dignified and confident manner in their dealings with colleagues and administrators. The list of common factors among referees who reached a high level looks formidable: formal training, experience, personal application, maturity, responsibility, integrity, good relationships, dignified bearing, good communication and confidence.

Whatever your motives for being involved in the game, whether as player, coach, administrator or referee, there is no doubt your actions on and off the field will truthfully reflect your inner feelings for the sport.

Those are the successful officials. All served an apprenticeship in junior soccer. Those accepted onto the FIFA list of international referees are required to add diplomacy and linguistic ability to these qualities.

Although my comments have concentrated on top officials, they can be applied to all levels. If there are any heroes in the game, they must surely include the thousands of referees who have faint chance to reach the top. Men and women who are content to devote a large slice of their lives to the service of the game at a grass roots level contribute much to the community.

Spirit of
the Game

In the Introduction, I mentioned recognition of referees who have a feel for the game, who want it played to the spirit as well as the letter of the rules. The vital difference is the depth of inherent passion that can enrich a performance. The same applies to performances by champion ice skaters, musicians, actors — in fact, all forms of human endeavor.

In the search for personal improvement, soccer referees can get very verbal when rummaging through the letter of the officials laws of the game. Just one word can spark a long and minute analysis of meaning and interpretation in play.

During those debates, a vital factor is often overlooked. That factor was spelled out by the International Football Association Board (IFAB) in a statement issued in Dubrovnik in 1968. It read: "The IFAB received many suggestions for improving the game and alterations to the laws, and such suggestions were carefully studied. It is the belief of the board, however, that the spirit in that the game is played is of paramount importance and that changes in the laws to improve the game as a spectacle are of little value if fair play is not universally observed."

The spirit of the game is of paramount importance. Words of wisdom, worthy of repetition. An appeal to keep the spirit above all other considerations cannot be ignored. It is an appeal to all who take part in soccer whether as players, coaches, match officials or as administrators,

What is the special significance of that phrase to the referee? What is your role in its interpretation and application? What is meant by the spirit of the game? If it is so important, it should be clearly understood so that we work together from a common base.

Is it some misty, intangible aura that surrounds those thousands of dry and dusty words that form the 17 laws? Or is it something that can be defined in such a way that those same words become vital, alive,

meaningful signposts to the heart of the game? To find the spirit, the first place to look is the beginnings of the modem game and analyze the basic principles that were locked into the first laws by the founders of what has become such a passionate pastime for millions.

What is meant by the spirit of the game? If it is so important, it should be clearly understood so that we work together from a common base.

A simple key can unlock those principles from those many cold legalistic phrases, giving to the bare bones of everyday words the flesh and muscle, energy and vitality, that we see on the field of play.

The method of play. The Football Association (FA) was born in 1863. Until then there had been no universal code for conducting a game that had historical references stretching back more than 2,000 years. The rules of play in existence when the FA was founded varied from one school or college to another. When students moved to other universities, new rules had to be learned. Also, confusion arose when schools agreed to meet on the soccer field. Before a match could be played, the rules of each school had to be debated and agreement reached or a compromise set of rules drafted.

By the mid-19th century two distinct patterns of play emerged. Some colleges favored kicking and dribbling the ball with the feet. Other important institutions favored carrying the ball and permitted the tripping and hacking of opponents.

When the FA first met in 1863, it was intended to incorporate the most desirable features of both the dribbling and the handling codes. The choice was not easy, for feelings ran high among the two groups of protagonists who gathered in the gloom of oil lamps in the Freemason's Tavern, Great Queen Street, Lincoln's Inn Fields in London, on a cold, gray December day.

In 14 simple rules, known as the *Laws of the Game*, the FA spelled out the method of play. Since then many changes have been made to the wording of those laws, but the basic principles of play have survived — a lasting testimony to the wisdom of the founders of the modern game. There was no mention of the spirit in which the game should be played, highlighted 103 years later by the IFAB as being of paramount importance.

The chosen method of play, and subsequent changes of emphasis introduced by the game's legislators, provide pointers toward three underlying principles of the spirit of the game:

• **Equality.** The first principle is that all players have an equal opportunity to demonstrate individual skills. By outlawing acts of physical contact such as tripping, pushing and holding, that could be put under a general heading of unfair play, the game was transformed from an ancient, rough-and-tumble, violent and dangerous activity into a sport in which skill is admired and encouraged.

Physical strength and size are not prerequisite for an individual to be able to show skill. That point is easily demonstrated in the composition of modem soccer teams by glancing through the 2003 MLS rosters. Notice there was a 90-pound difference between the Chicago Fire's 230-pound Zach Thornton and teammate Seth Trembley's 140 pounds.

Players of small physical size can and do reach the highest level of competitive soccer. In most cases speed and maneuverability put small players on level terms with opponents of greater power and strength. Thus equality of opportunity is provided for players to demonstrate individual skills.

• **Safety.** The second principle, in contrast with the violence generated in ancient soccer, is the player's health must be

safeguarded in normal match play. Great care has been exercised in specifying the components — the field size and player's equipment — to reduce hazards and promote a healthy environment without restricting skill too severely.

• **Enjoyment.** The third principle is that the game should provide maximum pleasure for all who take part. To provide a framework within which soccer can continue to be an enjoyable experience, legislators have identified certain acts of behavior as unfair, unsporting or just plain unacceptable. Strict punishments are incorporated to make it unprofitable for those who choose to ignore the basic code of sporting behavior. The enjoyment of soccer owes much to the determination of past and present legislators to preserve that fundamental philosophy.

Equality, safety, enjoyment. Three simple words, three vital principles dovetailed into the laws. But how can they be seen at work within the many ordinary words that form the text of the laws?

How can we relate those worthy ideals to soccer laws? We need a key that will open the door to the minds of the ancient legislators who invented a game that has intoxicated the world.

For more than 140 years legislators have rethought, revised and rephrased the laws while ensuring the fundamental principles have remained intact.

The key. The key is a simple three letter word, a word that has driven more parents of anxious infants to distraction than any other: "Why?"

This is how it works: A statement is chosen from a law, the key word is applied and the statement is analyzed to discover how the basic principles of the spirit of the game are locked into it. Let's extract something from law 1 (The field of play). The law reads, "The field of play must be rectangular." Why? Can the game be played on a square field? Or on a field that is rectangular but with the goallines longer than the touchlines? Why should the law insist that "the length of the touchline must be greater than the length of the goalline"? Which basic principles apply in that statement?

Part of the fun of scrimmage games is improvisation. No need for a formally marked field. Any open space will do. Makeshift goals are formed from shoes, bags or whatever and we can play soccer.

However as the game proceeds, two situations arise to spoil most players' enjoyment. First, the ball is kicked far beyond the goals and fun time is lost getting it back. Second, and more irritating, two players contest possession way out to the right or left, excluding the rest from sharing the fun.

Enjoyment level drops as a result of no restriction out to the sides of the playing area. After all, one main object of playing is to put the ball into the target, the goal. All play, to remain interesting and enjoyable, should aim for that simple objective. Any factor encouraging the flow of play between the target areas contributes to enjoying the game. Thus, by insisting the field be rectangular, legislators have provided a practical example of the third principle of the spirit of the game — enjoyment.

An example of the second principle, safety, concerns the size of the field. When first specified, the field was a maximum of 200 yards long by 100 yards wide. In 1897, the maximum length was reduced to 130 yards. Apart from radically affecting the playing tactics and increasing the enjoyment of goal area activity, players' health was less severely taxed than when they played on the larger area. Readers who have taken part in small-sided games on a full-sized field have experienced the excessive physical effort required to maintain skill levels.

The requirement for flagposts to be "not less than 1.5 meters (five feet) high, with a nonpointed top" reduces the element of risk to players. Shorter posts would be dangerous.

By posing the key question, "Why?" to other parts of law 1 you can find more examples of the three principles at work.

Analyzing law 7, why is a soccer game divided into two periods? Why not one period of 90 minutes, or four of shorter duration? Is it simply to change direction so that influencing factors of wind, sun, surface slope, etc., are balanced during the second period? That satisfies the equality principle, but where are safety and enjoyment?

The effect of enjoyment is illustrated in the diagram. The vertical scale measures enjoyment level, the horizontal represents time.

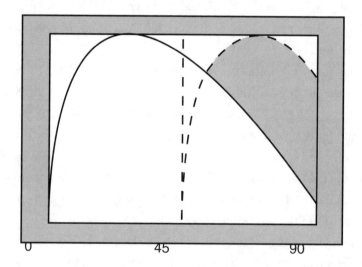

If a game is played non-stop for the full 90 minutes, the level of enjoyment should rise quickly when the players are fresh. It would then be expected to fall away rapidly as players become tired, lose concentration or patience and as level of performance deteriorates. Another childhood experience confirms that theory. Children will play soccer for hours non-stop until exhaustion overtakes their level of enjoyment.

By cutting the game into two periods and providing the players with a short interval to gather their energies for the second half, we expect the level of enjoyment will rise quickly to the peak achieved in the first period and that it will be maintained almost constantly until the end of play. Although players should be better able to cope physically with shorter periods, say four, their extra effort is likely to be countered by time lost in building to peak performance after the second and third breaks.

Law 7 provides equality in sharing the allotted time in the direction of play; safety, by providing an interval to reduce fatigue, and enjoyment to its theoretical maximum by playing two periods.

The ball. "The ball is ... spherical." Why? Can we not play the game with a cube- or a can-shaped ball? Certainly. Most readers have enjoyed soccer games with cans. Similarly, other shapes can serve as the ball.

A paper cup may appear to be taking that point too far, but a personal experience in South Africa suggests otherwise. At a soccer skills tournament for schoolboys at the Orlando Stadium, Soweto, boys demonstrated their skills by moving a ball, with feet or head, around an obstacle course. The tournament was interesting, but of equal fascination was a soccer match in progress behind one goal, where 30 to 40 contestants

We need a key that will open the door to the minds of the ancient legislators who invented a game that has intoxicated the world.

who had either completed their test or were waiting to be called, were generating much excitement and pleasure playing with a paper cup.

What are the special qualities of a sphere? Which basic principles of the spirit of the game are observed by that requirement?

Watch any group of children with a ball — it is never still, is constantly on the move from hand to hand, being bounced, thrown

or kicked from one to another. A ball is a friendly object, smooth to the touch, rolls when pushed and returns if properly treated. We find magic in creating dynamic situations with an inanimate object. Could a cube hold the same fascination? No. If it were pushed, it would stop; if dropped, it would not bounce. By comparison it is a lifeless, uninteresting object.

> **A ball is a friendly object, smooth to the touch, rolls when pushed and returns if properly treated. We find magic in creating dynamic situations with an inanimate object.**

The ball measures and reproduces the skills of the player. It is the only object that provides the player with an equal opportunity to demonstrate his skill — the definition of the first principle of equality.

The second principle, safety, is in the construction of soccer balls from "leather or other suitable material." Balls need to meet strict quality controls imposed by the International Football Association Board (IFAB), that reinforce safety standards. For the final principle of enjoyment, just look into the eyes of a child with a soccer ball.

Why offside? Can we play soccer without that controversial law? We did when we were kids. We knew nothing about the technical application and didn't want a referee to stop our game. What we didn't like was the kid who stood by the goal, ready to pop the ball in, without joining the team effort to get the ball there. It wasn't right; the kid was cheating. Some basic instinct taught us that soccer was more enjoyable if all players contributed to team play. In the Eton College rules of 1862 that guy was a "sneak."

On further analysis an offside rule (accepted in other team games) demands alertness, tactical intelligence. It contributes to fluid and attractive play and has transformed soccer from a mob scramble to a thinking player's game. Without it soccer would resemble ping-pong and reduce skills. So it encourages equality and demonstrates skill and adds to enjoyment.

Can that be right? The offside rule adds to the enjoyment of soccer? Yes!

Fouls and misconduct. Do we need that law? Why? Forms of soccer were played for centuries without it but where was the skill? Buried in violence and confusion. Law 12, by defining acts of unfair play, provides all players with an equal chance to demonstrate skills (equality).

No player enjoys being on the receiving end of excessive physical contact; the game deteriorates if impeding is not controlled or if goalkeepers are allowed unreasonable ball possession or indulge in timewasting tactics.

By encouraging skillful play, protecting players and providing an environment for sportsmanship, the law clearly echoes the spirit of the game.

The referees. Why laws 5 and 6? Does soccer need you? No! Not for scrimmage games played for fun in which the players decide what's fair and unfair. Not even for early English college matches played to a well-understood code of gentlemanly conduct.

You became necessary when the ogre of competition appeared. The need to win gradually suffocated the moral code. Disputed points mushroomed to force legislators to appoint neutral officials to decide and guide the play within the rules.

Today you have enormous authority amounting to total control. The advantage clause allows you the privilege to set aside the written rule and apply your interpretation of the spirit of the game.

Spirit of the Game

Today you have enormous authority amounting to total control. The advantage clause allows you the privilege to set aside the written rule and apply your interpretation of the spirit of the game. By discouraging and punishing foul play you provide the equality principle, allowing players to express skills. By surveying game equipment, caring for injured players and controlling temperaments, you apply the safety principle.

Above all, by your dedication to see fair play survive in the competitive world, you create a sporting environment at every game where the players, the laws and all connected with the event can obtain maximum enjoyment.

"The spirit of the game is of paramount importance." That is just as true today as when the IFAB proclaimed it in 1968. We've blown away the dust on the text and read between the lines to expose the inner soul of soccer.

You will not always have a written solution to a match problem. It is often said, "When in doubt, apply law 18: common sense." I prefer, "When in doubt, apply law 0: The spirit of the game," because it precedes and shapes the written law.

Ball Power

N ow, to the spirit and the written rules in practice.

"Here's the match ball, ref."

"Thanks," you reply, giving it the old two-thumbs squeeze. "Fine, let's go."

Hold on! Is that all?

In your hands is an object that will have an influence on the next two hours of your life. It deserves more than a cursory glance before you start the match.

What is a ball? Such a simple object but, what power! It can spark a fire in the eyes of a child, set a dog's tail wagging and put a smile on any sad face between Los Angeles and Boston!

Consider also, in a World Cup year, the power of a ball to focus the attention of billions on one sporting event for a whole month. That innocent-looking object has influenced the growth of national economies, affected political history and continually provides fantasy relief in a troubled world.

No one religion can motivate human emotions and actions as effectively as the sight of a soccer ball in play. What power!

For most of us the fascination of a ball started at baby stage and the moment we were first put on the floor to crawl. We began a great adventure into life, making two wonderful discoveries:

• Independence to move freely. During our first steps on a long journey a brightly colored round thing attracted special curiosity. We touched it and it moved, it rolled, it bounced. Exciting, fascinating!

• Physical power. The power to bring an inanimate object alive with our own hands and feet. Smooth, pleasant to handle, a ball became a friend for life, a partner in games – baseball, soccer, tennis, golf, hockey, basketball, etc. – in which we test physical and mental ability as individuals or in team play.

Pleasures of ball games stem from good organization, sensible rules and interaction with others. The focal point is the ball and what it is doing. We are riveted by its movement, whether induced by favorite players at the Rose Bowl, Yankee Stadium, Flushing Meadows or in the parks.

Pleasures of ball games stem from good organization, sensible rules and interaction with others. The focal point is the ball and what it is doing.

A ball mirrors the player's skills providing a constant flow of information in the form of signals.

What kind of signals? A famous golf teacher, John Jacobs, says, "The ball is your best instructor." To prove his point he would stand with his back to a pupil, study the flight of the ball and suggest adjustments for better performance. He gives two reasons.

"First, the ball is truthful and honest. It tells you what your club head is doing at impact. Second, the ball does not care about technique. However you hold or swing the club, your shots for good or bad are determined by conditions built-in at impact.

"A snap of the fingers is enough time for a golf ball to absorb, measure and reproduce skill input of direction, trajectory, spin, distance and roll."

A third factor may be added: neutrality. In competitive play a ball favors neither one player nor team over the other.

In soccer the ball transmits many signals to be read and interpreted. What are they saying to you, the referee? How can they help you to make the right decisions and take correct actions in every match?

A game of soccer boils down to two elements – the ball is either stationary (dead) or moving (live). From my own detailed research of hundreds of games, in different countries and at different skill levels, the ball is dead an average of 136 times in amateur matches and 108 at the pro level. Play is stopped by the referee 43 times per game in amateur play, 45 in pro 45. The ball goes over the boundary lines 93 times in amateur play, 63 in pro.

Higher skill levels at pro level and enclosed pitches explain the big difference in boundary line figures.

The ball is dead for free kicks (43), throw-ins (55), goal kicks (19), plus a few each for corners, kickoffs and offside.

A dead ball poses questions: "How did I get here? Who put me here?
How do I get back into play? Should I be kicked or thrown? Am I in the right position for the restart? Are players the correct distance from me? Are you, referee, in a good position to see my next moves?"

All simple questions, mostly answered automatically, but any wrong answers will affect the quality of your performance.

When the ball is in motion, you make hundreds of assessments and decisions based on reactions between players and ball. As with a golf ball, a soccer ball behaves according to impact conditions induced by the players. It reproduces skill input truthfully and honestly, without caring about technique and is quite neutral.

Behavior of your match ball depends on three factors: ball condition, conditions of play and player input.

Ball condition. Recall your law 5 duty to "ensure that the ball meets with the requirements of law 2." Hardly necessary now when FIFA-licensed balls cover shape, material, size and weight. What's left? Only pressure.

Soccer is the only ball game in which the match official may vary the ball condition. What criteria do you use to determine suitability for play? Just the two-thumbs squeeze? Is that good enough with an 80 percent margin between minimum and maximum pressure?

Ball Power

What is the objective? It is to provide a ball that will help the players to express skills to the best of their ability. Whatever affects ball behavior affects the results of player input and the quality of play.

Conditions of play. For your match, law 2 offers no guidance. But clearly, ball behavior will relate to surface conditions whether natural or artificial, soft, hard, dry, uneven, wet, snow covered or frozen. It relates to climate; cold or heat, rain, wind strength and direction. Any or all can affect the quality of play.

Player input. When the ball is live, player input starts with an assessment of ball movement — direction, speed, height, bounce, roll — followed by a calculation of what the player can do within personal skill limitations. Then a decision on action, programming impact conditions, carrying through to execution, and finally, observation of skill achievement. All in a second or two.

Even star players have problems with unpredictable ball behavior that provokes annoying errors of judgment. Incidents of dangerous play, mistimed tackles, ball-to-hand contact and out-of-play stoppages occur more frequently and players become frustrated. The quality of play suffers and your task of match control is made more difficult.

Observations noted during many top matches up to 1998 suggested that one in 10 were spoiled as a spectacle because the ball was not prepared to suit match conditions. During the first rounds of the 1998 World Cup, an alarming one in four were affected by a fixed ball pressure for all matches on firm surfaces. For later matches, referees were advised to be more thoughtful about ball condition with a marked reduction in ball behavior problems.

During and after the tournament star players, including Carlos Roberto, David Seaman, Deschamps and Barthez, were critical of unusual ball behavior. Carlos Roberto claimed, "The ball ruined years of hard work for me. My most dangerous weapon is to swing at free kicks. The balls soar out of control if you try to bend them." Seaman and Barthez had trouble reading long-range shots.

Even before the 2002 Japan/Korea World Cup, top players went public with similar criticisms of the ball chosen for the tournament. Fortunately FIFA recognized the excessive bounce problem and provided excellent pitch surfaces to absorb energy at impact. In just a handful of matches, players needed two touches to control awkward bounces, but in many games shots on goal were way off target. Some top players blamed the ball.

Maybe those comments were intended to cover errors, but neutral observations tend to back their views that more thought is needed in ball design to help players play to their skills.

Modern footballs are high-tech products usually made from synthetic materials. Some have thick outer casings incorporating micro gas-filled bubbles intended to soften heading feel, but also to produce explosive reaction to compression at impact. Generally they need high internal pressure to fill non-stretch skins and can be difficult to control on hard surfaces.

When the ball is in motion, you make hundreds of assessments and decisions based on reactions between players and ball. As with a golf ball, a soccer ball behaves according to impact conditions induced by the players.

They fly faster and farther than old leather balls and have changed the tempo of play with increasing use of long-ball tactics. Exciting for the fans but more frequent goalkeeper to goalkeeper exchanges can be boring, particularly on short pitches. On larger fields, referees need sharp mobility to get into good positions near to the estimated

dropping zones of long punts from goalkeepers and free kicks. Efficient support from colleagues on the line is critical if you are left behind play.

For your games, you cannot rely on quality surfaces. Arrive in good time to assess the surface and climatic conditions. If you have more than one ball available, choose low and high pressures and test on the pitch for feel, roll, bounce, etc. Think of player comfort more than law 2. A sound general rule is hard surface equals soft ball; soft surface equals hard ball.

On larger fields, referees need sharp mobility to get into good positions near to the estimated dropping zones of long punts from goalkeepers and free-kicks.

Check ball signals early. Is the ball bouncing unusually high? Is the second bounce as high as the first? Is the ball often airborne out of reasonable control? Note problems of ball control within the skill level available. Do talented players need two touches to bring the ball under control? Watch for mistimed tackles, ball-to-hand, dangerous play, frequent heading duels and head collisions, frustration, retaliation. Listen for players comments which may bear on ball behavior.

Ask yourself, "Is the ball right for this game?" Don't wait for halftime if the ball needs attention or changing.

Every player wants to play well, to enjoy the game and not get hurt. You can contribute positively to those simple aims by providing a ball that allows full skill input and satisfaction of achievement. By so doing you will reduce the need for disciplinary measures for everyone's enjoyment.

The match ball is your friend and partner, worth more than a two-thumbs squeeze.

Reading the
Game

Being "in the right place at the right time" shapes destinies, touching on career opportunities, meeting a life partner or making a crucial call in a soccer game. Where is the "right place" and when is the "right time" to make that perfect call? You can't rely on chance to decide. You can narrow your options by studying how to "read the game."

That may imply something written just as a script is prepared for a theatrical play. While every soccer game has elements similar to a play (i.e., stage, actors, directors), the script provides only an outline of the performance. The actual events to take place in the first and second acts are a mystery; heroes and villains are unknown until the final curtain.

Because every soccer match is a unique performance, no two matches can produce the same scenario — not even with identical players and officials. The most expert soccer analyst cannot forecast the play. Who could have imagined, for example, that Jack Taylor, the referee of the 1974 World Cup final, would award a penalty kick in the first minute, or that a second penalty kick would turn the fortunes of the game at a critical stage?

The uncertainty of a soccer game is one of its major attractions. But where does that leave you, the supervisor and director of the play? What guidance will help you deal instantly with unpredictable events?

Let's examine the factors that influence reading ability and suggest how you can develop your own ability to serve soccer better.

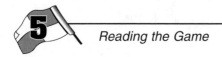

PREDETERMINED FACTORS

Some factors influence control before the game starts. You have to accept them as they are, but by careful observation and analysis you can program ideas into your match control policy. The predetermined factors are the system of control (such as the diagonal system of control, or DSC), ability of assistant referees, field size, surface conditions, weather, match importance and players' attitude.

DSC and assistant referees. The system of control is dictated by the authority responsible for your match. Depending on the authority, you may be the sole decision-maker or one of a two-referee team. Which ever version applies, you need to respect certain techniques that influence where you move around the field to find that "right place, right time" spot to make quick and correct decisions.

Even in the two-referee system, you are still concerned with good positioning. If you are the sole official (no neutral assistants) you'll have carte blanche to work out field coverage strategy.

If you have two neutral assistants, you are dependent on their ability to carry out assigned tasks. Their unknown ability is a "reading" factor as the game proceeds. Poor cooperation from assistants means less delegation of responsibility and higher mobility to observe play.

With two assistants you'll be operating in the DSC. It's worth realizing that system is intended to keep the zone of play between you and one assistant as you move along a diagonal path. That is not a rigid "train on a railroad" patrol. Experienced officials favor the presence-lends-authority approach. The closer to the incident, the better the control. Research in Japan on referee's movement produced two contrasting diagrams:

Figure 1

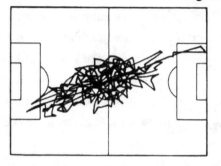

The diagram shows the path of an inexperienced, non-mobile referee. The narrow patrol path and the allegiance to the center of the field spell poor game control.

Figure 2

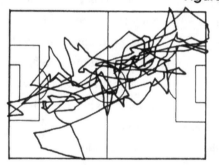

An international referee noted for fitness and hustle, that path keeps the referee close to play and varies the angles for observing players in various situation. That match had superb control.

Field size. If the field is small, you are likely to interfere with play in midfield. Consider adjusting the patrol by remaining nearer the touchlines. More goal-area incidents are likely because of the shorter distance between the goals. The smaller playing area is likely to mean more offside problems because of less space for the players to keep clear of active play zones.

On a large field you will need more help from assistant referees with calls for offside at quick-breaking movements, in placing the ball at free kicks close to the opposite touchline and in respecting the required distance at free kicks.

It is generally advisable to run directly into a low sun so that your head is turned to observe the play. The effect of the sun's position during latter stages of the game should be assessed before deciding which diagonal to run.

Surface condition. Wet, dry, soft, hard, level or uneven surfaces will influence the choice of footwear and cleats to provide optimum mobility.

If the field slopes from one corner diagonally across to the other, it may assist control to run the same diagonal across the slope throughout the game rather than running with and against the slope. Where the field slopes sharply but evenly from one end to the other, difficulty will be experienced in reaching the upside half at quick-breaking movements and you will need more assistance from the upside assistant. A very wet surface requires particular alertness because players will have problems in maintaining balance and timing tackles.

Weather. The direction and strength of sun, wind or rain are obvious influences on how a game may shape up.

At a top pro match played on an early summer evening, the referee made no allowance for the sun's position and chose a diagonal that meant that looking directly into a low, brilliant sun. In the opening minutes the referee missed two vital penalty area signals from an assistant while blinded by the glare. The referee had an extremely difficult match after those incidents.

It is generally advisable to run directly into a low sun so that your head is turned to observe the play. The effect of the sun's position during latter stages of the game should be assessed before deciding which diagonal to run.

A strong wind blowing from goal to goal will affect positioning at goalkicks, free kicks and punts by goalkeepers, and may incur delay in retrieving the ball. A spare ball kept near the down-side goal may be a wise precaution. If the strong wind is across the field, more touchline incidents are likely to occur on one side. Station the more experienced assistant on that touchline.

Match importance. Some matches are more important than others. The first state cup match is as important to a new referee as the first international match is to the official with many years of experience. An extra check over pregame factors will help confidence.

Take nothing for granted — even routine matters normally left to others. Remember the start of the 1974 World Cup Final was delayed because corner flags were not in place. The referee for the 1982 World Cup match between Brazil and Argentina did not spot that all 22 players were wearing socks of identical colors. Those and many other experiences confirm the wisdom of taking that little extra care with the preliminaries to every match, whatever its importance.

Players' attitude. Players' attitudes before the kickoff will be conditioned by many influences. Domestic problems, unhealed injuries, previous encounters between the teams, coaching instructions and "big game" nerves all can show in early behavior patterns affecting your control strategy.

Check out the predetermined factors as far as you can. In time they will become automatic reading elements for all matches. Keen observation and analysis will prepare you for the unscripted 90 minutes that follow.

FACTORS WITHIN YOUR CONTROL

Factors that are within your control and can be developed are knowledge, experience, psychology and mobility.

Knowledge of the laws. Constantly review each law and International Football Association Board (IFAB) decision. Keep up to date with annual law changes. Study FIFA World Cup memoranda. Organize a personal library of works on soccer and match control. Discuss problem laws, such as the advantage clause, with other officials.

Refined law knowledge is vital. It is an error to assume that, once qualified, further study is unnecessary. The laws change and although the changes are seldom of a major character, make it your business to keep up to date with the changes announced by the IFAB. Sources for that information are FIFA, the United States Soccer Federation, state and local referee committees. Attend their meetings.

A memorandum prepared by the FIFA Referees Committee for the conduct of the final stages of each World Cup championship sets the world standard. The first memorandum was prepared during the course of the 1966 World Cup in England. It provided guidance on a day-to-day basis for the 31 officials employed in controlling 32 matches within 20 days.

A personal library is a must. Historical works on the beginnings of the modern game provide a deeper understanding of the laws. They cover such subjects as the origins of the laws, the practical problems in play that led to changes and experiments with new versions of the laws. Books written by referees will include many practical experiences of value. Weekly and monthly sports magazines will keep you up to date with trends in soccer. Views on law applications by players, coaches and others, plus published articles with a special interest to match control, will be worth extracting and filing away for quick reference.

Discussing problem laws with colleagues is excellent for extending knowledge. In the process of such discussions you learn about your own attitude to the game. Specific topics on which regular discussion is advisable are the advantage clause of law 5, offside and practical interpretations of unusual types of fouls or misconduct related to law 12.

Knowledge of the game. Play the game. Watch matches live or on television. Study officials' positioning at live- and dead-ball situations. Note recurring problems, particularly at free kicks and corner kicks. Study wall formations and control problems. Note unusual variations of delay tactics at free kicks. Note the changing character of the match relative to the score. Note the influence of the touchline and the methods used. Note the influence of substitutes.

Playing soccer is invaluable to appreciate players' attitudes, movements and skills. It's also great fun. Short-half, small-sided scrimmages are learning opportunities. Watch as many games as you can. Officials' positioning at dead balls is easy to observe and assess. When the ball is live, make a conscious effort to note the positions of the officials. There is always some point of interest for a serious referee to relate observed game events with personal match control ideas.

The changing character of a match affects the game-reading process. Weather variations will influence the game, particularly if starting dry and finishing wet; the changing score will promote different degrees of player urgency; the introduction of substitutes; injuries to key players; the interchanging of positions — all will have some influence on the pattern of play and can be studied with interest. Glance occasionally at the coach to note how instructions

Reading the Game

are given and the effect on the individual players in terms of closer marking of opponents, stronger tackling or position changes. How do those relate to reading the play?

Knowledge of skills. Study the basic playing skills of balance and control. Note mannerisms — for example, those of one-sided players. Note methods of screening the ball. Note mannerisms in jumping for the ball by goalkeepers and other players. Note the goalkeeper's handling techniques. Note the use of the arm in natural balance and the differences when pushing an opponent. Observe the rate of acceleration, change of pace and direction. Knowledge of skills enables the referee to read the player's intention when in control of the ball and to anticipate the next move more accurately.

Some players are "one-sided," that is, they favor either the left or the right side to control the ball. Argentina's Maradona, a strong left-side player, was one world-class player in that category. The apparent handicap of not being "two-footed" calls for exceptional balance to maneuver the ball onto the favored side. The manner in which a player positions himself relative to the ball will give the observant referee a clue to the next action, e.g., the direction of a pass, a screening movement or a shot at goal.

A feature of modern soccer is the use of a hand or arm to fend off opponents as seen in figure 3.

Figure 3

In many instances that is fair, using the arm as a cushion to reduce the impact of an oncoming opponent. But some players, while apparently concentrating on controlling the ball, extend the hand or arm to push the opponent. The difference is not always easy to detect, particularly when a player fends and pushes in one movement An experienced observer will learn to judge the fairness of movements.

Players' mannerisms in jumping for the ball are important in striker-versus-central-defender challenges. The defender is usually a tall player who may appear awkward when jumping for a high ball and is unfairly punished for what is for him a natural movement. However, some tall defenders unfairly restrict the challenge of an opponent by extending their arms over the other's shoulders — in effect, holding him down, as seen in figure 4.

Figure 4

Taller defender holding an opponent

There are forwards who appear to jump for the ball when their intention is to jump into the opponent. Alternatively they may make little attempt to contact the ball but back into the opponent

Reading the Game

(making a back) so the opponent appears to be unfairly impeding, as seen in figure 5.

Figure 5

Making a back or moving under an airborne opponent

To pick out the player who has a natural awkward action in jumping from another who intentionally impedes his opponent, make a mental note of the natural action when not under pressure from a challenging opponent.

Speed and acceleration of players are worth noting, particularly among front players. You may need that knowledge to avoid being stranded at a quick counterattack. Intelligent assessment of players' off-ball positioning will alert you to sudden direction changes and to dangers of interfering.

To sum up what to look for in player skills, read and reread the FIFA analysis of one master craftsman:

"Johan Cruyff has unique physical attributes — a lean, powerful frame with long legs. Like all elusive forward players, he possesses fast muscle, capable of quick reaction and contraction. He can stop and start more quickly than opponents, which gives him scope to avoid a tackle, dodge

past a player and race or out jump him to the ball. His endurance enables him to work incessantly throughout the game, moving first in attack then in defense, dribbling to create an opening or running off the ball to help a colleague. Then he is gifted with high skill in techniques, deft in his ball control and sensitively accurate in his passing. He is everywhere getting involved in the play, taking corners and free kicks and then positioning himself away from the ball to create a diversion as a start to a new phase of play."

EXPERIENCE

Quantity of experience. Experience will provide reference points to which play situations can be related in order to achieve good positions. The quantity of experience, in terms of the number of matches in which the official participates, is clearly fundamental to the learning curve. Officials who seek every opportunity to referee as many matches as is practical will improve reading ability more quickly than those who control the occasional organized match. Small-sided games, five- or six-a-side, practice matches and scrimmages all have their value as sources of match points to add to the store of knowledge.

Quality of experience. Quality of experience will depend on the area in which the referee lives. In some areas quality competition will be very limited. In others, particularly in large cities, the range will cover school competition through professional soccer. Where it is possible to serve more than one competition, new referees are advised to broaden experience by applying to serve several levels. As officials learn and demonstrate ability, it will follow that they will be qualified to participate in more senior soccer and move up to officiate at the highest levels of the game.

In the context of quality of experience, it is essential to gain experience of higher levels of soccer by serving first as an assistant referee. Valuable knowledge will be gained looking at match situations from a different vantage point. In addition, being on the touchline provides opportunities to meet and observe more senior officials in action and to discuss the particular incidents that occur during the matches served.

A personal library is a must. Historical works on the beginnings of the modern game provide a deeper understanding of the laws.

Own experience. The most difficult task in assessing one's own performance is to be objective. It is too easy to blame others for problems that have occurred. In some instances that may be valid, but on reflection some incidents may have been directly or indirectly influenced by one's own shortcomings. At the end of each match when the excitement of play has cooled down, an analysis will not only serve to judge the standard of performance during that game but will also provide points on which further study and effort are needed to improve future performance.

It is not always easy to remember exact moments of play because of the speed of movement, the intensity of factors to be read simultaneously and the unknown outcome of a particular piece of play. However, a start can be made by trying to relate important decisions to the positions from which they were taken. Each goal is a reference point. Ask yourself simple questions such as: Where was I when the goal was scored? Was I in a good position to observe play immediately before the ball entered the goal? Did I check with my assistant referee before signaling the goal?

Was there any protest from the defending players? What was the nature of the protest (for example, offside)? Could I have been in a better position to be certain my decision was right? If so, what can I learn from that problem?

Was I too far away from play? Too close to play? Too far ahead or behind? Would my decision have been better accepted if I had been in a better position? Where would that position have been? Was it possible for me to have been there? Why was I not there?

Similar questions can be applied to the positions from which penalty kick, offside, free kick and corner kick decisions were given.

What problems were experienced with players, club officials or spectators? Consider problems that arose with individuals. What was the nature of each problem? How did it arise? Did I observe clearly the source of the problem? Could I have been better positioned?

Problems with assistant referees: disagreements on the direction of a kick or throw-in. Was I at fault? Why? Did I agree with all offside indications? If not, why not? Was I in the best position to confirm or deny? Did the assistant referees carry out my instructions? If not, were my instructions clear? Can they be improved?

Did I have any problems when the ball was put into play from goalkicks, corner kicks, free kicks and throw-ins? For example, did I find myself interfering with play by taking up a bad position? Have I experienced similar problems? What can I do to find a solution?

Objectivity can be increased if it is assumed that there is at least one learning point in every match and that the analysis is directed toward finding the problem from which the point arises. It is likely that several learning points will be discovered in the process. It is refreshing to hear referees of many years' experience, at the very top level of the game, admitting that they are still learning the art of match control.

Reading the Game

Experience of others. Learning from others is a lifelong experience. Learning what should not be done is often given more emphasis than learning what should be done. In many instances that is just as valuable because the advice is based on mistakes committed by others, sometimes at considerable personal expense. People who are prepared to admit they made a mistake are worth listening to because they are being objective and are prepared to accept possible ridicule in order to help others who might make a similar error. Seeking out such match officials will be rewarding for the inexperienced referee. A great deal can be learned in a short time by discussing practical match incidents with them. That the decision of the referee is final, as stated in law 5, is as it should be in the interest of sportsmanship. It does not mean the decision is always correct.

The key to efficient decision-making is position. Knowing about positioning mistakes is part of the way toward knowing the better positions. Top officials voice concern that at certain stages of play they have found themselves in bad positions. For example, in the DSC the referee sometimes finds himself interfering with play. The referee may be struck by the ball or impede players. The DSC itself is often blamed, but more objectively the referee has not read the signs accurately or has not been mobile enough to keep clear of play.

Ball-watching is another reason for bad positions. Coaches work hard to train ball-watchers to resist their natural instincts and concentrate on the movements of colleagues and opponents when the ball is in flight. Similarly, a referee who has problems keeping clear of play should consider whether slow movement to better vantage points is caused by concentrating too long on the ball.

Noting match trends can be helpful to good positioning. In my experience, a fairly regular pattern appeared over many professional matches. The most difficult period to control appeared about 10 minutes after the start of the second half and lasted about 15 minutes; that is, between the 55th and 70th minutes.

Exchanging experiences of cheating and gamesmanship ploys must add to knowledge and alert the referee to situations which can change moods, patterns of play and positioning.

PSYCHOLOGY

Own psychology. Your psychological make-up and personality will directly influence your actions on the field.

Your attitude to the game will also bear directly on the manner in which you deal with incidents. Others will react according to the way in which your actions impose on their approach to the game.

Studying their reactions will provide a mirror to your own mental approach. For example, to treat all players as criminals is to invite criminal reactions. To treat them as human beings is to invite responsible human behavior; that is a sign of mutual respect and confidence that is observed by the vast majority of players. When major incidents occur in a match it may not always be entirely the fault of the individuals concerned. An analysis of the build-up to such incidents may indicate flaws in your attitude. For example, were you being dictatorial or arrogant? Did that spark a chain of inflammatory events? An official with an exaggerated idea of his position in the game will be blind to signs of ill-temper caused by an overbearing and objectionable personality. When emotions

Officials who seek every opportunity to referee as many matches as is practical will improve reading ability more quickly than those who control the occasional organized match.

overflow, that official will often be out of position and be required to take more strict action than would have been necessary if his attitude had been less unyielding.

Psychological preparation for a match is as important as ensuring that you have packed your shoes. An international level referee due to officiate a top pro game realized he left his kit at home after driving for an hour. He returned, collected his bag and rushed to the stadium.

Objectivity can be increased if it is assumed that there is at least one learning point in every match and that the analysis is directed toward finding the problem from which the point arises.

By kickoff time he expended much nervous energy and was not mentally prepared for his task. Within the first minutes his positioning was badly at fault and two fouls went unpunished. He never recovered full control of that match.

Psychological preparation begins the moment the match appointment is received even though the match may be days or weeks ahead. No matter how unimportant the match may be, it is a commitment in your diary and in your mind. Going through the preliminaries of exchanging correspondence with the club, planning the route to the stadium and preparing and packing the match kit will increase the nervous anticipation of the test to come, just like the build up to an examination. If any factor, such as the unfortunate incident mentioned above, should break down the degree of mental preparation, the referee who appreciates the value of being in good psychological condition will attempt to regain lost ground before the kickoff.

Self-confidence is a variable mental condition. It is extremely rare for an individual to remain self-confident for an indefinite period for the simple reason that the factors that make up self-confidence are variable.

Knowledge of the game, of match control, is never complete. Referees can never be sure they will be able to cope with an entirely new experience. Obviously, the more knowledge officials accumulate, the greater will be their confidence to meet new situations. Physical and mental conditions vary according to such factors as environment, state of general health, domestic or business problems, and affect the level of self-confidence at any given moment.

In positioning during play the level of self-confidence will be an important factor. A hesitant official with a low level of confidence will have more problems finding the right positions than an official with a high level of confidence. The latter will decide quickly where to be and will move sharply to that position with the knowledge that, if it should need adjustment, the referee has the mental alertness and the confidence to make the right assessment.

What can be done to achieve a high level of self-confidence before a match? Apart from accumulated knowledge and experience, probably the best advice is to pay careful attention to personal grooming. Public relation experts drum that into clients because a neat, tidy appearance attracts interest and respect. Witness presentations of royalty, politicians and military personnel and note their superb appearance.

Lift low spirits on a bad day by taking extra care with your own appearance. Recall that you represent not only yourself but the soccer authority that assigned you to the game.

Others' psychology. Essentially your task is to manage people. To be successful you need to have some idea of the make-up and psychology of other people, to recognize their personality types and to know what motivates them.

Understanding people is halfway toward managing them. Understanding players is halfway toward being in the right position at the right time to manage a situation on the field of play.

We have seen that a player's attitude before the kickoff is conditioned by many influences. As the referee you will not know that the small, innocent-looking number 11 of the red team had a violent argument with a loved one just before arriving at the match and is looking for the first opportunity to express those inner frustrations. You will not realize that the goalkeeper of the blue team remembers that the ache in an ankle is the result of a deliberate kick received from the opponent's number 10 when the same teams played three weeks ago. However, the alert official will quickly recognize symptoms in those players that suggest their psychological condition is unstable. It may be necessary to adjust positions during play to be close at hand should they lose emotional control. A word of advice to "cool down" offered at the right psychological moment can be enough to keep such players out of trouble and the match under sensible control.

It is said that personality changes with environment. How true that is can be observed in thousands of ways at a big match. The small, harmless, timid person in the street is transformed into a dancing, shouting, demoniac extrovert inside the soccer stadium. So often players who have aggressive attitudes on the field are perfect citizens away from it. Referees have to deal with personalities as they present themselves on the field, not with what they may know them to be in normal daily life. There are many stories of referees who have found it necessary to dismiss players who are great personal friends — an interesting confirmation that the referee puts love of the game before love of a friend.

Practically all players are motivated by the simple enjoyment of kicking a ball about with friends, by the desire to express themselves through their skills and to experience the healthy pleasures of physical exercise. They enter the field looking forward to a good match. As we have seen, that simple ambition can be frustrated according to the environment in which the game is played. It is the referee's duty to control the environment so that a sporting contest ensues.

It is natural for players to express their feelings when a goal is scored by their team. The environment will dictate the manner in which those feelings are expressed. It may be unseemly for grown men to hug and kiss after a vital goal is scored, but it is understandable in the same way as our quiet friend in the street will give vent to his feelings in the stadium environment. Conversely, reactions to vital goals scored against are often excessive, particularly if players see the possibility of a reprieve because of a supposed infringement by the opponents before scoring. Such excesses of emotion are accepted up to a point. You have to judge the moment when they go beyond reasonable bounds within the context of each match and take whatever action is necessary to restore equilibrium. It is often the case that a quick but firm word is

Knowledge of the game, of match control, is never complete. Referee can never be sure they will be able to cope with an entirely new experience.

enough to break the glassy stare in the eyes of an over-excited player and bring him back to Earth.

First, you need to be aware of the different personalities you will face during play; second, recognize symptoms of psychological instability; and third, put yourself in a position where you can exercise a calming or, if necessary, a disciplinary influence.

MOBILITY

Strictly speaking mobility is not a reading factor. It is the means of putting into effect the results of the reading factors previously discussed. Without excellent mobility the hard work of assessing reading factors will count for little. For example, assessing a situation from your deep knowledge of the game, using first-class understanding of the players' psychology, you may decide to move your position 40 yards to the right. But if your mobility is poor you may not reach the right position at the right time to observe the anticipated incident. The result could be guesswork.

GENERAL FITNESS

Good mobility stems from general fitness. A few simple points should suffice here to stress the need for attention to general health.

Refereeing is an athletic activity. It is common sense that athletes who wishes to perform the activity well should begin by assessing their basic state of health and then take positive action to improve deficiencies and develop whatever physical and mental requirements are necessary for his tasks.

Mental fitness. An alert, active mind is essential for good refereeing because visual problems are being fed into the brain at high speed. The process of registering a situation through the eyes — for example, the positions and movement of players at a corner kick and the direction, height and speed of the ball — is followed by the measurement of the action against the referee's understanding of the laws; the balancing of the answer with a tactical situation (possible advantage); the formulation of a course of action and the transmission of signals from the brain to the body to carry out that action — all in a split second.

How can an official improve mental alertness? Attention to the previous comments on general health is the starting point. Checking current alertness by simple tests is the next step.

One simple test is to describe aloud all visual information received by the eyes during a short car journey, such as the general scene, kind of road, what the cars in front and behind are doing, what traffic is approaching, pedestrians about to walk into the road, a car overtaking. Relate that to the actions which follow the mental assessment of the situation, for example, the need to change gears, brake, accelerate, operate indicator lights and the many hundreds of operations that are repeated in different order throughout the journey. The speed of assessment and the associated physical movements will give an indication of the mental alertness of the driver. One thing is certain, the driver will not be able to deliver the words quickly enough to keep pace with the mental and physical gymnastics of making decisions and carrying out the actions.

Mental alertness can be improved by sharpening your powers of observation. For example, police trainees are given brief glimpses of a number of objects for a few seconds and then asked to give a detailed description of as many as possible. Or, describe people in a photograph — shapes, sizes, clothes worn, colors, etc. Such mental exercises can be enjoyable as well as constructive.

Physical fitness. What level of physical development do you need? The short answer is whatever is necessary to enable you to move around the field to keep in close touch with a fast-moving game without undue strain.

An alert, active mind is essential for good refereeing because visual problems are being fed into the brain at high speed. The process of registering a situation through the eyes – for example, the positions and movement of players at a corner kick and the direction, height and speed of the ball – is followed by the measurement of the action against the referee's understanding of the laws ...

How do you achieve a satisfactory level of physical fitness? There is no short answer to that question because every official will require individual advice depending on the general state of health and existing physical capabilities. Individual training is a matter for experienced physical therapists to plan and monitor. If you are fortunate enough to have access to qualified therapists at a local club or gymnasium, or a referee colleague employed in physical training, you are well advised to take advantage of such services.

Basically then, you need to concentrate on acceleration, speed, ability to maneuver and stamina. Most officials will have little difficulty in finding somewhere to run — a local sports track, park, forest or road — in order to develop all four requirements.

Adopt a daily personal physical routine that includes deep breathing, bending and stretching exercises, pushups, jogging, running and sprinting. The aim should be to progressively increase the level of performance until a satisfactory standard has been achieved. That may take several weeks depending on the initial condition. Many officials play other sports that develop and maintain physical condition. Sports that demand coordination of observation, assessment of situations, speed of decision and physical action are particularly appropriate for the soccer referee. Such sports include tennis, squash, badminton, basketball, volleyball, table tennis, water polo and, of course, soccer itself.

Excellent mobility is a great asset if used intelligently. It can get you to the right position at the right time to make that perfect call.

Summary. Every soccer game is a play performed just once and without a script. What the 22 performers will do is a mystery. Each has his own part in the play and appears from time to time but the director, the referee, is required to control the action every second. The enjoyment of the players and the audience depends a great deal on the success or failure of the referee to stay out of the scene until direction is needed. The referee must have the ability to read situations accurately and to give intelligent direction quickly so that the story can continue to interest.

How to develop reading ability has been the subject of this chapter. It is presented as a framework within which you can develop your own ability to read the predetermined factors and to make the best use of knowledge, experience and psychology with good mobility. Apart from helping you read the game, close study of some of the subjects, particularly playing skills, will bring new interest and pleasure into your task. Attention to physical and mental preparation will not only improve your ability to control soccer matches, it will develop personality and confidence in meeting the problems of daily life.

Gamesmanship
or Cheating?

Humorist and author Stephen Potter describes gamesmanship as, "The art of winning without actually cheating."

Gamesmanship has become a common word in the sports world. Potter invented and defined the term, which has a ring of mischievous fun. It's a popular term for small acts carried out during a sporting contest intended to put opponents off their stroke or gain an unfair advantage. "Small acts" because, to keep within the humorous limits of the word, they should not appear too serious, disconcert the opponent too much or gain too unfair an advantage.

A slight noise, a cough or the rustle of paper, say in a game of pool or golf, may be enough to force an opponent's error. To qualify as gamesmanship the action must appear accidental so the intention behind it can be disguised. The opponent is suspicious but can never be sure the distraction was intentional, particularly if the distracter apologizes for disturbing that concentration. The damage has been done. The shot is missed and the incident is then classified as "all part of the game." The term implies an unavoidable and unlucky break, such as the unexpected bounce off an uneven surface that causes a player to mis-time a play.

If gamesmanship becomes more intimidating, repeated to unfairly influence the whole play, calculated and rehearsed with willful intention, the humorous and mischievous connotation of the word disappears. It is replaced by a more serious and distasteful word — cheating. Few athletes will be upset if accused of gamesmanship, but to be accused of cheating is intolerable because any success achieved in a career will be flawed.

There is no clear dividing line between gamesmanship and cheating. The common link is the intention to gain an unfair advantage, clearly contrary to the spirit of the game. Because it is your duty to safeguard that spirit, it follows, you need to be aware of what acts of gamesmanship or cheating may arise in matches, just as you need to recognize fouls and misconduct defined in the laws.

The term "gamesmanship" is used throughout this chapter because of its general acceptance in the game. However, you will recognize determined attempts to cheat.

Background. Gamesmanship is not new in soccer. It started in the 1890s when the players' right to appeal for decisions was abolished. The referee was charged with discipline and game control, with power to punish what he considered intentional fouls and to dismiss players.

By that time professional soccer was established and growing. Paid players began to demonstrate skill not only with the ball but also in preventing opponents from scoring by committing deliberate fouls or by stopping the ball with the hands. The latter was directly responsible for the introduction of the penalty kick in 1891. Those and similar acts became known as "professional fouls." Relationships between players and referees cooled. The referee, an amateur, became the person to outwit. Because the referee represented authority, an undetected foul or an action that gained an unfair advantage was considered a victory against authority and "fair game."

> **The referee, an amateur, became the person to outwit. Because the referee represented authority, an undetected foul or an action that gained an unfair advantage was considered a victory against authority and "fair game."**

The same attitude applies today and is called gamesmanship. The only difference today is the acts of gamesmanship are more numerous and sophisticated in character.

Not long ago a well-respected team manager in England shocked an audience of referees by declaring, "I have to teach my players to be five moves ahead of the referee." Maybe he was exaggerating to make his point, but the message was unmistakable.

The term "professional foul" was probably meant to imply that such actions would only be committed by a low-paid professional in order to keep a job. At that time the true sporting game was amateur soccer. It was not of much concern that a few professionals, out of the thousand or so employed, should commit such ill-mannered and ungentlemanly acts. In one sense, the situation has not changed in that professional fouls are committed by a small percentage of all soccer players. What has changed alarmingly, however, is the effect of those actions on soccer as a whole and on the referee's task in particular due to great advances in communication.

Specific acts of gamesmanship, cheating or professional fouls, whatever label you wish to give them, can be observed in junior soccer within 24 hours of being seen on television. Recently an eight-year-old boy returned home after playing for his team and was heard to boast that he had committed "a pro foul" on an opponent to stop a goal. His justification was that he had seen his professional idol do the same thing a week earlier. Referees report examples of dissent by young players that, a few years ago, were unheard of. One referee reported having to dismiss his own son for swearing during a friendly match.

Gamesmanship, then, started when soccer became competitive. Considerations of employment and monetary rewards, prestige and glory, achievement of social positions beyond normal expectancy, have all been factors contributing to the growth of what has been described as the cancer of soccer. The exciting skills of talented players have too often been blunted, submerged or even annihilated by willfully constructed practices. The basic principles of fair play are of no concern to those who contrive to win at all costs.

Some say top-level soccer will always be played with gamesmanship because the rewards of success are so dazzling. False. Witness the world's best players competing in the 1990 and 1994 World Cup Final tournaments in Italy and the United States, respectively. There can be no higher acclaim for an individual than world acknowledgment of his skill and sportsmanship. Such sportsmanship and entertainment were possible only due to the determination of FIFA to present soccer at its best, with rigid control, and to the cooperation of the team officials and players. If such results can be achieved at the highest level they can, with similar determination and cooperation, be achieved throughout the game.

To be effective, gamesmanship needs planning. For the must-win-at-all-costs coach it pays to know what strategies will make that fine-line difference between win, draw and lose.

Apart from team selection and match tactics, every successful gamesmanship ploy is money in the bank. In the coaches' "Gamesmanship" dossier, we expect to see major headings such as referees, time wasting, free kicks (theirs/ours), intimidation, off-ball items, dead-ball and live-ball situations, etc. There will be subheadings such as "Objective" (what we want to achieve) and "Action" (the ploy). Against each sub item might be a value. There will be many 10-cent entries, several solid earners and some potential $1,000 bonus matchwinners!

Are those an exaggeration? No! Not when fortunes can be at stake. That is known as "being professional." The dossiers can be copious depending on how professional the author wants to be. New items are added after each gamesmanship brainstorm meeting.

Objective	Action
10-cent entry	
REFEREES – Check out the ref before match starts. Is he going to catch the small items? If not, he could be influenced on the big ones.	1. Kickoff. Put player over half line in other half. If ref lets it go we try all items. If not, try items 7,8,10.
Good earners bracket	
FREE-KICKS – (theirs) Front of our goal. Neutralize defense.	1. Create delay to reform defense. 2. Try wall at six yards. 3. Block kick. Delegate quick player to attack ball before kicked. Rick is allowed a yellow card
$1,000 match winners	

PENALTY KICKS – Just one could be enough!	1. Rehearse induced fouls:
	
	    a. push off and fall
	
	    b. trailing leg "trip"
	
	    c. hip "trip" falls
	
	    d. trips over own feet

One tasty nugget is recounted by Norman Burtenshaw in his book, *Whose Side are You On, Ref?* Leeds United versus Birmingham, 1972. At the pregame field inspection, Norman meets a visiting player measuring the field length. "One half is six yards longer than the other," he says. "My manager got me to check because they've pulled that stunt before. It helps their players with positioning for offside." In the '70s Leeds was well-known for being "super professional."

Because the rewards are irresistible, the world sees gamesmanship ploys in practically every televised game. Is it surprising to see young and adult players trying the same tricks?

How to limit gamesmanship? Knowledge. No one knows all the tricks — no one ever will — but you can prepare yourself to combat gamesmanship by making your own dossier — become more "professional!" Wherever you are in the soccer refereeing hierarchy, you have already experienced some acts of gamesmanship. You've had problems with defense walls, encroaching at free kicks, false claims for free kicks, corners, throw-ins, etc.

Because the rewards are irrestible, the world sees gamesmanship ploys in practically every televised game. Is it surprising to see young and adult players trying the same tricks?

In the course of your career, say 1,000 games, you will accumulate knowledge of, say, 50 different acts. One hundred referees will each experience a similar number but, of the total of 5,000, probably 90 percent will be common. That means 500 different acts are spread among individual referees.

Ideally, those should be collated and pooled to all match officials. Impossible, perhaps, but here are four suggestions to increase your own count:

• Personal observation. At every game, look for new ploys. Register play situations where gamesmanship occurs or is likely to occur.

• Share experiences. Meet with other officials, discuss match incidents regularly in groups. Give and receive.

• Instructors' dossier. Instructors can contribute by maintaining a dossier of gamesmanship acts for the instruction of new officials. Dossiers can be compared with other instructors and expanded from group meeting.

• Practical demonstrations. Those are very effective in small groups on a soccer field. Groups are allocated situations, free kicks, penalty kicks, etc., to expose known ploys and to rehearse a few for demonstration to the whole assembly in the appropriate location. All ploys are recorded. Questions and discussion promote advice from leaders. The final report to all serves as a personal dossier for future extension.

Such a session is very instructive and good fun for all.

Referees are innocents abroad compared with the professional approach of elements with vested interests. You can never hope to be one move ahead of the determined cheats, but by extending your knowledge you will not only be better prepared for future games, you will not be five moves behind.

Your Tactical
Bank Account

If coaches consider successful gamesmanship ploys as money in the bank, think about opening your own account with the title, "Soccer Tactics."

Why? Why should you be concerned with game tactics? The short answer is for better match control. Applying tactical knowledge to assess game situations and predicting the next phase of play will guide you to the right position to make correct decisions. It's all part of reading the game.

Soccer tactics vary from the "kick-and-rush" of kids, following the ball as a swarm of bees follows its queen, to highly sophisticated systems employed at the international level.

Youth players may not plan tactical play but every match has its tactical calls, be they from the players themselves, coaches, parents or involved fans. Young Jimmy or Sarah are constantly urged to "drop back," "hold the ball," "mark number 10 tight," etc. Most of the advice will fall on deaf ears, but an alert referee will be listening and looking for closer physical contact between marking and marked players.

Tactical advice may lead to nothing more than a few fair challenges. Fine, but be aware of the aggressive defender who is encouraged to attempt a series of unfair tackles you can nip in the bud.

At higher levels, with more at stake, match officials must have an in-depth knowledge of soccer tactics. Coaches often critique referees who appear unable to read deliberate destroying tactics against key players. At the extreme, coaches will alter team selection based on the referee for the match. Top referees are under the coaches' microscope before every match. An official noted for a lenient approach could be a danger to a highly talented and sensitive player who may not be risked against an opponent renowned for provocative tactics. It happens. Just as coaches plan game strategy, you can formulate your own with built-in tactical know-how. Add a refining touch to your judgment or positioning for those instant gut reaction decisions. How? In a nutshell, seek and thou shall find.

It's a big subject; witness the extensive coverage of soccer tactics in written and visual forms. A great deal of tactical discussion is highly theoretical and tends to confuse rather than enlighten. Unless you want a coaching license, you don't need to have an opinion on comparing the 4-2-4 system with the 4-3-3 or the "total football" approach practiced by the Dutch national team in the 1970s. Your concern is what is likely to appear in front of you in your next match.

The wealth in your bank account of tactical know-how depends on what you put into it and what you can beg, borrow or steal from others. Your own contributions will rely on observation. The rest will depend on what you can transfer from the accounts of others already rich in tactical wealth.

Open your account by studying tactics at matches you watch live, on video or on television. Simplify the task by splitting the account into live-ball play and dead-ball restarts.

Live-ball play. Note basic team formations and the functions of specific players. Identify the key players with special skills for winning the ball, control in possession, the player to whom the ball is distributed and the key attacker with a flair for beating opponents on the ground or in the air. Assess the general style of play of each team, i.e., reliance on power, speed and technical skills. Note change of formations when the ball is lost to the opposing team. Put yourself in the position of the player with the ball and assess options available for dribbling, running, passing, shooting, etc. How does the player solve the problem of what to do next? What are teammates and opponents doing in the immediate playing area? Extend your horizon to take in off-ball incidents. Listen to tactical advice and assess reactions.

Look for offside tactics, i.e., defenders moving forward. Note good and bad positioning by match officials to survey offside situations. What type of marking tactics are employed, i.e., man-to-man, zone or a combination of both? Does a team favor long-ball passes or possession play? What is the goalkeeper's part in team tactics, i.e., long punt, throws out of defense or sorties out of the penalty area?

Deposit into your bank account observations on how game conditions affect tactics; changes in weather, surface condition, effects on play caused by injuries, substitutions and change of score. There's never a dull moment in building a useful balance in your live-ball account.

Dead-ball restarts. All restart situations offer a mine of tactical treasures. Free kicks, especially near a goal, throw-ins and corner kicks make up the main subheadings in that account. About 40 percent of goals result from those situations. The coaches know it and plan offensive and counter offensive tactics that are easier to assess because the match is stopped. There's time to study player setups, particularly at defensive walls, where the match officials are positioned and the immediate tactics when the ball is put into play.

Coaches often critique referees who appear unable to read deliberate destroying tactics against key players. At the extreme, coaches will alter team selection based on the referee for the match.

Transfers from other accounts. How are you going to beg, borrow or steal from accounts rich in tactical wealth? We're talking about experts, most of whom are only too willing to transfer their tactical cash. How to touch that jackpot?

For a start, operate on the principle that if you can't beat them, join them. You could take a coaching course. Apart from learning the theory and how it's put into practice, your own input based on your refereeing experience would be much appreciated. Otherwise, close contact with individual coaches or coaching associations will present opportunities to discuss tactical play.

If you officiate mainly youth soccer, don't imagine that better knowledge of tactics is not really necessary.

Persuade your referee association to invite well-respected coaches for a presentation of their view and exchange of ideas for the good of the game. There is special value in attending refereeing courses that include practical field demonstrations of soccer tactics, with input from well-experienced referees and coaches. It is important to gain knowledge about positive tactics so that a constructive ploy is not unwittingly frustrated, e.g., tactics to beat the offside trap.

If you officiate mainly youth soccer, don't imagine that better knowledge of tactics is not really necessary. Tactical coaching is growing fast. Some relatively simple tactics observed in television games are copied in youth soccer. Those appear mainly at dead-ball situations; you should know them.

At whatever level, consider the impact of coaching on the pattern of play in the second period. If you've had a good first period reading tactical situations be prepared to see a new game after the coaches have had their say during the break. Treat every match as two separate half games.

Finally, keep your tactical bank account up-to-date — your bank manager is watching.

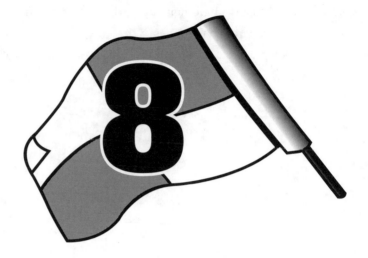

Deal the Cards

The World Cup provided one of soccer's most historic matches on July 23, 1966. England and Argentina, both unbeaten after three preliminary rounds, readied to do battle at London's Wembley Stadium for a place in the semis. The match promised drama and it delivered.

One of 90,584 fans at the stadium, I sat behind the Royal Box in company with 25 other off-duty World Cup referees from the British Isles, Europe, South America, Asia — the four corners of the globe. My fellows included an Arab army general and an Israeli at a time of high tension between their respective homelands, but soccer was the first priority during the three-week tournament.

Wembley never looked better with its lush green turf bathed in brilliant sunshine. A scarlet uniformed military band marched and countermarched across the sacred arena, thumping out popular tunes to the whistling and singing, good-humored crowd. Song sheets, scarves, hats, anything in hand, were waved in the prematch fiesta. The scene was ready for the actors to play their parts. Argentina was in blue and white vertical stripes with black shorts. England was in all white. Between the teams stood the match officials, Rudy Kreitlein of Germany and his linesmen, Godfried Dienst of Switzerland and Istvan Zsolt of Hungary, all clad in traditional funereal black.

As the band stopped and prepared to march away, the first sign of trouble appeared. Each team had four soccer balls for a warmup kickabout, but two Argentines broke ranks, ran to the England lineup, appropriated two balls and sprinted back toward their warmup goal. England players, hands on hips, looked bemused, hunched their shoulders and decided to get on with the kickabout. Already, the Argentines were winning by six balls to two!

Thirty-six minutes into the match, the game's central confrontation took place. Kreitlein, a slight, dapper, strictly correct official, was in a standoff with the towering Argentine captain Antonio Rattin. Rattin was protesting allowances he believed the officials were giving English players. Kreitlein's bald head, reflecting the sun, bobbed in animated discussion. He was clearly upset with Rattin's attitude, even if he couldn't understand the Spanish coming from Rattin's mouth. Suddenly, Kreitlein pointed to the dressing room, ordering Rattin off.

Pandemonium broke out. The referee was immediately surrounded by blue and white shirts as teammates tried to get Rattin off the hook. England's players stood by and watched. The Argentine group moved to the touchline to argue with interpreters, team delegates and FIFA officials. The late Ken Aston, ex-international referee and then-head of the FIFA referees' committee, used his height, weight and powers of persuasion to quell the argument but time continued to tick off the clock. The crowd slowly clapped and sang, "Why are we waiting?" to the tune of "Oh, Come All Ye Faithful." I looked at the other World Cup referees. All were on the edge of their seats wondering what they would do in Kreitlein's place.

> **The referee was immediately surrounded by blue and white shirts as teammates tried to get Rattin off the hook.**

Could this be the first walk-off by an international team? At Wembley, of all places? It was a disgrace in those days to even be cautioned at Wembley. Unbelievably, it seemed that Kreitlein had changed his mind. Rattin turned away and re-entered the field. I was now out of my seat, fuming with rage. At that moment I vowed to forsake soccer forever if Rattin didn't walk. I was halfway to the exit when I turned to see Rattin being led away. Justice prevailed after all, but it had been a long seven minutes.

The Sunday morning papers ran banner headlines. "Go Home, Thugs!" and "Animals!" they screamed, repeating a comment by Alf Ramsey, the usually passive England manager. Press reports revealed violent postgame incidents. Kreitlein was assaulted by Argentine players. FIFA's match commissar, Harry Cavan, was spat upon.

Another problem surfaced in the press. Brothers Bobby and Jackie Charlton, England's heroes, read that they had been cautioned by Kreitlein during play. The referee was quoted as saying, "I had to caution them for ungentlemanly conduct," but the brothers denied any knowledge of being disciplined.

FIFA went into an emergency huddle and issued a severely worded statement accusing Argentine players and officials of bringing the game into disrepute. The Argentine Football Association was fined a derisory $150 (the maximum allowed by FIFA statutes) and threatened with exclusion from the 1970 World Cup tournament. Rattin was banned for four international matches and two other players got three-match bans for assaults on FIFA officials. "Powder puff punishment," cried the media. The statement also confirmed the cautions on the Charlton brothers. "The ban is savage," Rattin fumed. "England must be allowed to win the World Cup. The referees are on their side. I only asked the referee for an interpreter."

Out of the unsavory episode was born a positive and historic soccer innovation. The inability of the German referee to communicate verbally with the players was at the heart of the problem.

Out of the unsavory episode was born a positive and historic soccer innovation. The inability of the German referee to communicate verbally with the players was at the heart of the problem. Aston, one of the most respected soccer educators of our time, pondered that as he drove home after an arduous spell of World Cup duty. It seemed that every traffic light was against him. Yellow — caution. Red — stop. Yellow — caution. Red — stop. "That's it!" decided Aston. "We'll try colored cards for cautions and dismissals."

The card system was introduced at the opening game of the 1970 World Cup finals (Mexico vs. Russia). German referee Kurt Tschenscher produced the first yellow card to caution Russia's Asatiani for foul play. It came out again four times in the match and an average of once per match for the total 32 matches. Not one red card was seen, although it's been very visible since.

Despite its painful conception from the confusion of that game in 1966, the card system has grown into a universally understood method of communicating disciplinary action.

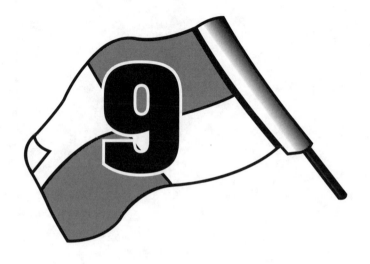

The Trial and Triumph of Esse Baharmast

On June 23, 1998, in Marseilles, France, U.S. credibility in world soccer hung by a slender thread. The national men's soccer team, already defeated by Germany and Iran, was still two days away from defeat at the hands of Yugoslavia, but the prospect of salvaging some respect at France '98 was slim. Responsibility to raise spirits in the American camp rested on the shoulders of just one U.S. citizen, Esse Baharmast. Baharmast, the nation's top soccer referee, would be in charge of the Brazil-Norway match that decided the fate of placings in Group A. Brazil was dry with two victories, but Norway had to win to finish ahead of Morocco. It was going to be a tough game needing tight control.

Baharmast had achieved more than any other U.S. referee ever had in being assigned to two tournament matches. A good game would put him in line for one of the climax matches — maybe even the final.

Brazil at full strength is a sight to behold anytime. That night was no exception. The Scandinavians dug deep to keep a clean sheet, a scoreless game, until the 77th minute when Brazil's Denilson juked his way past three defenders to make scoring a simple task for teammate Bebeto. Five minutes later, Norway's Tore Flo tied the score with a brilliant solo effort to make Norwegians believe in a miracle.

With just two minutes to play, Baharmast whistled a penalty against Brazil. Why? It was not clear but the referee's body language suggested a holding offense. The South Americans protested but, strangely, without conviction. Up to that moment Baharmast had kept the game disciplined, showing two yellow cards in the second half. Norway scored from the penalty to send Brazil to its first defeat in the World Cup since Italy '90 when it lost,

1-0, to Argentina. Norway played David to Brazil's Goliath and advanced to the second round to face Italy.

Coming so dramatically late in the game, the decisive penalty call was a natural discussion topic among the media. On the way to his dressing room, Baharmast crossed paths with Michel Platini, president of the French Organizing Committee. "A good penalty decision, referee," Platini reportedly said. Zico, the Brazilian assistant coach, had accepted that the call was correct to Michel Vautrot, representing the FIFA referees committee. Baharmast was congratulated by his match colleagues and was proud to have contributed a positive image for U.S. soccer.

Trial

Fast forward two days later, to Manoir de Gressy, 25 miles east of Paris, FIFA's headquarters for World Cup referees. It was early morning and Baharmast was in a state of shock. He had been crucified by the world's media. Because Norway won the match, thus eliminating Morocco from the tournament, a deluge of accusations reported on television, radio and in the papers ranged from incompetence to racism to being a pawn in a European soccer hierarchy plot to deny African ambitions in the world sport. His penalty decision was widely described as "imaginary,"

With just two minutes to play, Baharmast whistled a penalty against Brazil. Why? It was not clear but the referee's body language suggested a holding offense.

"ridiculous," and "a cruel injustice to Morocco," eliminated because of Norway's win and on its way home. There were cries for investigations and protests to FIFA to change the result or replay the match. The soccer world was abuzz with the media hysteria. Baharmast knew the truth but was advised not to get embroiled in a mudslinging match with the media. He was in tears, helpless, and his career hopes seemed ruined. He felt he had brought shame on the 105,000 U.S. referee corps and cast another shadow over the American soccer scene.

"The FIFA referee committee was very supportive," Baharmast later recalled. "The other referees came to console me. They, too, felt the pain. I received many messages, by phone, fax and e-mail from my family and friends back home saying they trusted and believed in me. They had no doubt I had made the right decision. Even with all that support, I could not believe what was going on. It was a living nightmare.

"In the last minute of a game, if I'm going to call a penalty kick, it's not going to be an imaginary penalty," Baharmast declared.

At the International Media Center (CIM) in Paris, at a late-morning press conference, David Will, then-chairman of the FIFA referee committee, stated that the committee had seen evidence that confirmed the penalty call as correct. A Swedish television camera had caught the action from a different angle than the official images had shown and it could be viewed on a Norwegian television website. A rush to computers produced a photo showing Brazilian Junior Baiano clearly puling down Flo to prevent him from reaching a pass in the penalty area. A later sequence showed the full action from grabbing Flo's shirt to falling. The penalty was incontestable.

> "In the last minute of a game, if I'm going to call a penalty kick, it's not going to be an imaginary penalty," Baharmast declared.

The conference audience had represented an important but small section of the huge media presence at France '98. Reuters put out a rush item vindicating Baharmast that the French national television

station included in its 1 p.m. news program. It was not seen at the
CIM, where most of the rest of the world's media was preparing
dispatches on the first-stage results. Clearly they had to know, and
quickly, that a monumental injustice had been heaped on Baharmast.

Having seen first-hand when I was president of the Football
League Referees Association in England how malicious media
assaults on defenseless officials can wreck the lives and ambitions of
honest men, I became angry. As a coordinator of information for the
press at the CIM, I felt it was my duty to put the situation frankly
that the media had judged and crucified Baharmast without evidence
of a crime. Here was an opportunity to regain
some of the eroded dignity of the journalistic
profession by admitting a serious error and
offering an unqualified apology to the victim.
I wrote a printed appeal, distributed with a
copy of the website publication, to all the
media, including individual reporters. The
reaction was immediate and positive with
many promises to redress the situation. From

FIFA's confidence in Baharmast was confirmed when he appeared as the fourth official in the quarterfinal later that week.

past experience with certain sections of the media I was not
optimistic that those promises would be kept. Fortunately, I was
wrong.

Triumph

The next day, in Manoir de Gressy, laudatory bells were ringing
for Baharmast from the first light. Television stations covered the
story in depth. "Yes, it was a penalty. The referee was right,"
repeated the commentators. "Sorry, Mr. Baharmast," splashed across
international headlines. "We were wrong. All our excuses to
Monsieur Baharmast," admitted Paris newspaper *Le Monde*.

"One French newspaper said (Baharmast) deserves the highest matches," said Will, "because he sees something that 16 cameras couldn't pick up." Those who could not face a full apology published the facts and complimented the referee. And so it went for a day or two. Baharmast was truly vindicated, at least by the media.

"I'm not angry," said Baharmast. "I sort of laugh at it now. Everything happens for a reason. It's the media that needs to back off and let the referees do their jobs. If we started picking on reporters for the mistakes they make, well, the amount is large in comparison to what we do."

FIFA's confidence in Baharmast was confirmed when he appeared as the fourth official in the quarterfinal later that week.

Despite and because of his highs and lows at the World Cup, Baharmast enjoyed a career year. On July 22, 1998, he was named USSF director of officials. He has since been named director of advanced and international referee development. Baharmast also completed his onfield career when he worked the center for the 1998 MLS All-Star game in Orlando, Fla.

Baharmast, already highly respected in America, survived the poisoned pens of the international media and thrived, virtually single-handedly vindicating American soccer on the world stage. No official in any sport in 1998 was put more to the test and came out as highly regarded.

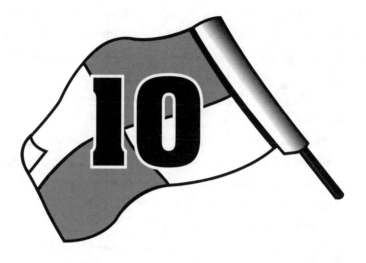

Show and Tell

FIFA president Joseph S. Blatter once said to me, "FIFA is like an old Victorian lady: very set in her ways and slow to accept new ideas." We were discussing the need for a simple code of signals to help referees communicate decisions to players and fans. When Brazil played France in the 1998 World Cup final before an audience of many millions, it is unbelievable that only one person, Moroccan referee Said Belqoia, knew the whole story of what went on in those 90 emotional minutes of play.

Most decisions for stopping the match were obvious, e.g., the ball going over the boundary lines, but others were obscure. We could only guess when a free kick was awarded in the run of play. It could have been for any one of many offenses listed in the official laws.

Soccer is often called "The People's Game" but there is an almost studied conspiracy of silence in helping the people understand their game. It stems from the Victorian principle, "What the people don't know won't hurt them."

Do the people care? Well, I'm one of them and I do care. An experience in China tells me I'm not alone. In my book, *Soccer Rules Explained*, I tell the story of a soccer match at The Workers Stadium, Peking, before 40,000 spectators. Most of the applause occurred when the action was stopped by the referee. An international referee seated at the halfway line gave a running commentary explaining why Doctor Wong, the man in the middle, had awarded free kicks. The people appreciated that insight into the game through the eyes of an expert and applauded the officials more than the players.

As a 14-year-old player, I was puzzled why the referee had called a fault against me, so I asked him, "What's that for, ref?" I'm sure I was not impolite but the answer, "Don't question my decisions; go on with the game or you'll be in my book," seemed unjust. I was not

contesting but asking for information to know what I had done to avoid repeating the offense.

After the match I asked the referee again, explaining why I wanted to know. He was more reasonable: "You put your foot up close to an opponent and I considered it to be dangerous play." I thanked him, adding that I would try to be more careful in the future. Then I thought, why didn't he show me at the moment by, say, raising one foot to knee height? I and all present would have understood immediately. So, the people want to know and the players want to know.

What about the media at the big games? As communicators, any tidbit of information eases their task of presenting the play, adding to the educational value of their output and, in turn, increasing the pleasure of the audience, as in that Peking match.

Other sports are way ahead of soccer in communication. Nearly all have an established code of signals to back their rules. Baseball, basketball, ice hockey, football, cricket and the rest all help explain what goes on. So, where's the problem in soccer, the world's most popular sports spectacle? One reason is that the game of Association Football (soccer) was created for gentlemen who imposed an impeccable code of fair play on themselves. The referee was there only "to decide disputed points" put to him by the players. Appeals of, "That was unfair, sir," and the accused villain's response of, "No, I don't think so, sir," were resolved by the neutral official. It was unthinkable that gentlemen should show dissent, by word or action, of any decision given by the referee (the second of the seven yellow card offenses in today's laws). The referee has never been required, officially, to explain or justify decisions because of that gentlemanly ethic — hence, no code of signals. Tradition dies hard in soccer.

Attempts to move tradition into the 21st century have, so far, produced little change. From personal research involving two years of study of referee communication, it is clear that officials want to be more informative. The only mandatory signal, to indicate that a free kick is indirect (law 13), could result from any one of a dozen offenses, from offside to unsporting behavior. To be helpful, referees use other signals on average 14 times per match. An analysis of six semiprofessional matches produced 27 different signals, falling into two categories.

What about the media at the big games? As communicators, any tidbit of information eases their task of presenting the play, adding to the educational value of their output and, in turn, increasing the pleasure of the audience, as in that Peking match.

• Instinctive (Natural gestures miming the offense, e.g., handling the ball, pushing, kicking an opponent, etc.).

• Contrived (Individual expression of offenses difficult to mime, e.g., impeding, offside, dangerous play, etc.).

Understanding varied according to the efficiency of the referee's body language. Those who attempted to communicate appeared more decisive than those who made scant effort. Often, negative reaction from players or viewers was stifled when a clear, firm signal was displayed. From that research, an unofficial experiment was tested at a national youth competition final at Crystal Palace, near London. Players and spectators were given a leaflet with diagrams showing referee signals they might see and what they would mean. The test was announced over the public address system before the kickoff. It was as near as we could get to the situation in the Peking match. It created much interest and was warmly received. A typical comment was, "Why can't we see that in every game?"

A paper detailing the research and the experiment was submitted to FIFA with recommendations for a basic code of signals for soccer. That was 1974. The old Victorian lady syndrome was clear in a memorandum, published in the *1977 FIFA Universal Guide for Referees*, which included the following: "It is not the duty of the referee nor is it a useful function to explain his decisions to the players or spectators. Any attempt to do so can lead to confusion, uncertainty and delay."

A slight change of attitude in 1991 led to the memorandum we now have. It repeats the fear of confusion, etc., but states: "There are times when a simple gesture ... can aid communication and assist toward greater understanding, and gaining more respect, to the mutual benefit of referees and players."

> **Miming and gestures that inform are no problem. They could be more widely encouraged, however, if illustrated in a guide to confirm the intention of those frequently observed.**

It makes no reference to the needs of the millions who watch and want to know more about their game, to the ever-growing numbers of newcomers attracted to soccer, nor why it is not possible to devise a simple code of signals to reduce the confusion, uncertainty and delay, ever present in this modem game.

Miming and gestures that inform are no problem. They could be more widely encouraged, however, if illustrated in a guide to confirm the intention of those frequently observed. The real value of a standard code would be to identify offenses difficult to mime and to decide on an appropriate signal. Examples are offside, dangerous play, impeding an opponent and a selection of the yellow and red card offenses. The first code could be minimal and tested, with adequate education, in a competition.

One of the FIFA president's first actions was to present an 11-point program to his executive committee. Point 10 reads, "Further improvement to refereeing standards with the aim of enabling referees to serve (soccer) more fully."

In discussions with referees at all levels, a code of signals has been welcomed with enthusiasm. They are keen to give it a try.

Blatter can score a winning goal for soccer people by encouraging referees to reveal their insight of the game. Now that we've entered the 21st century, it's time to bury the old Victorian lady.

Evaluating
World
Standards

The Class of France '98

Sixty-four international matches in 33 days is a lot of top-flight soccer. The World Cup is a unique showcase for the players to excite and thrill, a marvelous occasion to study the current state of world soccer officiating.

Does that concern you at your level of the game? Yes, most definitely, because you suffer more criticism and abuse every time your colleagues are presented in the media as "inconsistent," "morons," "incompetent little Hitlers," etc. The lone spectator at your games has read all that stuff, seen it on television and gives you hell. His huge dog bares its teeth in agreement, straining on the leash to get at your legs. You prefer that the top referees are shown as good people, just like you. If not, why not, and what is being done to promote the positive image of your role in soccer?

The 34 World Cup whistlers at France '98 came from as many different countries in Africa, Asia, North and South America and Europe. All are responsible citizens in government, education, medicine, finance and legal professions, with one essential common denominator — a passion for soccer. Five of those men officiated at USA '94.

How did they make out? FIFA rated their contribution at 8.30 out of 10 over the 64 matches. My own perception, based on analyzing 46 matches, was close at 8.32. Was that good, bad or indifferent? It depends on what you expect from a panel of international referees representing the best in the world at the most spectacular sports event of the decade. I see it as indifferent. Apart from the final rating for France '98, we need to study the trend. Is it improving, sliding or static?

Look at the diagram comparing ratings of World Cup officials since 1970. The highest (8.50) was achieved at Mexico '70 and Italia '90. The latter was considered satisfactory, given the increased complexity of play over two decades. USA '94 was disappointing

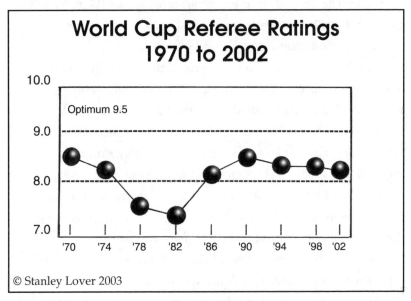

**World Cup Referee Ratings
1970 to 2002**

© Stanley Lover 2003

after much preparation by FIFA and the USSF. Putting France '98 into context, I gave the referees the same rating as USA '94 at 8.32. Conclusion? The trend is static.

What does that tell us? We are making no progress, running hard but standing still. Progress to where?

What should be the optimum target? Can we be satisfied with an efficiency of 85 percent? I think not. Players, fans — the whole sport — deserve better. Clearly, 100 percent efficiency in a human activity such as whistling soccer games is unobtainable. Should we not be working to achieve 95 percent efficiency? It can be done, but how?

Selection. The traditional method of selection relates to the relative strengths of soccer in the six FIFA Confederations. The 34

France '98 referees were spread thus: Asia, four; Africa, five; North America, three; South America, six; Oceania, one; and Europe, 15. According to my assessments, only seven (20 percent) rated 9.50 or higher. South American referees produced three; Asia, two; and North America and Europe, one each. More than a quarter of the 46 assessments recorded ratings of 7.00 or less.

Understandably, all Confederations wish to have a fair share of the places available on the World Cup panel. However, that does not guarantee a panel of the world's best officials for the world's best teams. Many observers have made the same point: The system of selection needs to change even if it means a Confederation is not represented and that several officials from the same country are appointed, if considered worthy.

Professional referees. From the beginnings of soccer, the system of employing "amateur" referees was adequate. Today it is not, at least at the World Cup level. Spiraling national, financial and medal ambitions focus on the most minute influences on match results. That puts an enormous burden on willing, but under-prepared, match officials. FIFA acknowledged that fact and, for more than 10 years, have encouraged national associations to introduce professional referees in their top leagues. The response has been slow and uncoordinated.

What could provide a dramatic and lasting solution would be the creation of a FIFA pool of professional referees employed only to control soccer matches at the international level.

What could provide a dramatic and lasting solution would be the creation of a FIFA pool of professional referees employed only to control soccer matches at the international level. Ten to 15 "Superefs," guided and administered by a well-qualified former

FIFA official, would find plenty of work in the 800 or so international matches played each year. They would travel the world, recognized as paid specialists and arrive at World Cup tournaments with the experience of more than 100 international matches behind them. Each official could control five or six matches with a more consistent performance than has been seen from panels of 30-plus assembled from as many countries. We could reasonably expect to eliminate the 7.00 and below ratings in favor of more 9.50s.

Their expertise would also be in demand for the benefit of aspiring successors and to promote the image of soccer officials at all levels. FIFA is the right and proper authority to set up a professionally managed service to coordinate, direct and develop a high standard of international match control. Recruitment is no problem. Some FIFA referees are already fulltime in the game with designations such as "civil servants," "sports advisors," "physical education teachers," etc.

I have met others ready to abandon careers to dedicate their lives to soccer officiating. Their employers are effectively subsidizing "business soccer" by allowing time off and accepting less than full attention to the needs of their own affairs. Where that flexibility is not available, officials compensate by sacrificing family vacation allowances. All for soccer.

Financing is no problem. Small cuts from match receipts, a few percent from the colossal World Cup incomes, fines imposed on those who abuse soccer discipline and some Swiss francs from the healthy FIFA coffers would add up to a sizable budget to ensure independence from subsidies and sponsorships.

In my study of match control at Mexico '86, I wrote: "At present, there is no coordination of instruction at the international level, no program of development. Without such a program, the match control aspect of (soccer) will decline because deficiencies will receive only patching-up attention. This will surely cancel much progress achieved in the coaching, administration and medical components of FIFA activity."

My report on USA '94 repeated that observation. It remained valid after France '98.

Class of Korea/Japan '02

What was different from previous tournaments and how did the officials rate?

No change in quantity of matches — 64 played in one month — this time spread between two countries, separated by the Sea of Japan, in 20 superb modern stadia. Inherent political, economical and geographical complications, and the need for tight security — a few months after Sept. 11, 2001 — encouraged forecasters of doom, but the event turned out to be a monumental success for the organizers. On a wave of a typically gracious welcome by millions of Asians it became a colorful spectacle of fair play and fun all the way.

FIFA expressed concern that mistakes had caused teams to complain, with some justification, and promised action to improve methods of training future officials.

Selection. No change here to the traditional lineup of officials, balanced out between the six FIFA confederations, with UEFA taking the lion's share — 14 each of the 33 referees and 33 assistants. No country had more than one referee or one assistant.

All were well prepared physically, following individual fitness programs devised by FIFA specialists. During the tournament every match was videotaped and analyzed for technical items and incidents of special interest to officials.

Discipline on the field, measured by 272 yellow and 17 red cards, showed a downturn on France '98. The good news is that the officials produced the best ever efficiency rating (9.05/10 based on 60 games), compared with personal studies covering the last nine World Cup final tournaments. Our diagram took an encouraging shift, indicating progress at last in world standards of match control.

The bad news is that a few glaring errors by a handful of referees and assistants were blown out of all proportion by the media (what's new?) to invite severe criticisms of overall performance. Replays of incidents proved officials correct in most cases, but when errors were clear to all, they tended to highlight inefficiencies of the established system of control.

FIFA expressed concern that mistakes had caused teams to complain, with some justification, and promised action to improve methods of training future officials. One immediate move brought a major reshuffle of the FIFA Referees' Committee to take a fresh look at the whole scene. FIFA frowns upon use of technological aids (except maybe sensors to survey ball-over-line situations), wishing to preserve the human element of the man in the middle as fundamental to the game.

Ball problems. Chapter 4 relates problems of unsuitably inflated balls observed during the 1998 World Cup in France. A vital factor was a fixed internal pressure reacting on field surfaces of variable condition, soft to hard.

In Korea and Japan, meticulous care in preparing the playing fields, to produce a fairly consistent softish feel, reduced excessive bounce. However, summaries from personal match observations show problems of overbounce in one of every six games and surprising errors of control and shooting in two of every five. The same criteria, as used in previous studies, were applied to this tournament.

In my view more attention is needed to the design and manufacture of high-tech footballs and matching the ball to game conditions on the day.

Video replays: To see or not to see? Supporters of video assistance for referees argue that, at the pro level, the traditional ethic, "The referee is always right even when proved to be wrong," is no longer relevant in a high-powered entertainment industry. Any factor that can distort a result, whether it be corruption, drugs, cheating, or referees "mistakes," demands serious attention. The stakes are too high to allow commercial objectives and ambitions to be frustrated by officials of variable competence.

To underline that view, the Italian chain RAI, which paid $80 millions for TV transmission rights at the 2002 World Cup, was reported to be considering a claim against FIFA for financial losses due to "referee errors" that, they said, put the Italian team out of the tournament and lost important publicity income.

Because it is physically impossible to see everything in a fast-moving game, the human referee will make "mistakes." He needs help. Some is provided by assistants and fourth officials, but with limited viewing angles.

Why deny the referee the advantages of video playbacks, available to millions, when he is the only person required to make correct decisions? When clear errors were shown on television a puzzled audience asked, "If we can see those errors, why can't the officials have access to the same visual information and get decisions right?" Such denial is like withholding vital evidence at a trial which could change a guilty verdict to non-guilty.

A soccer referee with a handheld video replay display is a logical development. Every pro game is stopped for over 100 in-play and out-of-play events. To check a major incident — referred by a qualified observer — would take no more time than a corner kick, goalkick, substitution, etc.

The introduction of professional referees has recognized their proper role in the game but "mistakes" continue to be highlighted on the screen.

Had video support been available during the 2002 World Cup, probably five or six results would have been different, more just.

World Cup Lessons – Helping Your Control

One of the most hotly debated decisions during France '98, particularly among supporters of the French team, was the red card shown to Laurent Blanc that barred him from the final match against Brazil.

We know that France won, 3-0, and not much more was said about the decision. Had France lost, Spanish semifinal referee Garcia Aranda would have been pilloried by the media for denying France its strongest lineup in the final. The referee earned top ratings for his handling of the semifinal, but the red card puzzled many colleagues. Television replays showed Blanc delivering a light, backhanded slap to the face of close-marking Slaven Bilic, Croatia's "hard man," just as a corner kick was about to be taken.

A regular feature of France '98 was the jostling between players at corner kicks, but we'll come back to that. Blanc "struck an opponent," a penal offense if committed "in a manner considered by the referee to be careless, reckless or using excessive force." In the days when that offense first appeared in the *Laws of the Game*, it was generally understood to mean a deliberate blow to the head or other body parts — an intolerable action deserving dismissal.

The "careless" and "reckless" qualifiers to the six penal offenses in today's laws are applied to thoughtless actions that put an opponent in personal danger. "Using excessive force" needs no explanation. Blanc's light slap does not fit well into any of those categories, so what was the offense? The contact occurred while the ball was out of play and deserved some disciplinary sanction. A yellow card for unsporting behavior could have been appropriate, a red card if the act was considered violent conduct. The key factor in that incident was Bilic's reaction, staggering backwards, hands clutched to his face in mortal agony. The referee had not seen what led to the confrontation and was persuaded by Bilic's acting that the player had been struck with excessive force, enough to be considered as violent conduct. Red card to Blanc.

Another factor that applied to all World Cup referees was the imposition of instructions by the FIFA referee committee before and during the final tournament. The general message was to be tough in interpreting foul play, particularly tackles from behind that endanger the safety of an opponent. A special video was shown to clarify acceptable and unacceptable challenges, but as the tournament progressed, the message seemed to change from, "You are being too lenient," to "You are over-reacting."

> **The key factor in that incident was Bilic's reaction, staggering backwards, hands clutched to his face in mortal agony. The referee had not seen what led to the confrontation ...**

A huge dossier of indiscipline — 258 yellow cards and 22 red — suggests a wide gap between players' and referees' interpretations of the way the game should be played. To narrow the gap requires much education and communication well before the final stages of the World Cup tournament. It should start from the first of the hundreds of qualifying matches, be monitored and shaped so that the players and officials arrive at the finals knowing exactly how the matches are to be played and controlled. It is unreasonable to expect officials of several years experience in top soccer to make important last-minute adjustments to their interpretations of play that, after all, got them selected to the world playoffs.

Corner kick supervision. The Blanc-Bilic incident arose at a corner kick. A common feature in most of the France '98 matches was corner kick aggressiveness. Coaches know that just one corner kick can decide the match, so they want their players to apply set plays in an attacking situation and counter with ploys to frustrate opponents' tactics when defending. Up to 20 players can be milling around in front of the goal while contesting for position and space: holding, pushing, blocking, shirt-tugging, any action to get an advantage. Inevitably, tempers flare and can lead to a Blanc-Bilic flash point.

The disappointing aspect of match control in France '98 was that so much aggravation was tolerated and seen by millions of players who believe it is a normal part of the game. They copy the top pros in the games you officiate, adding to your task. That's disappointing, because most corner kick tactics can be snuffed before they get out of hand at any level of soccer. If you don't have a plan for corner kick situations, the following will help you reduce your problems.

• From the instant you award the corner, observe and follow the attackers' movements coming forward and watch defenders dropping back. Look for close marking and observe any move to block the goalkeeper.

• Be visible. Move smartly to a position where the players can see you watching. At the first sign of an aggressive move, get in close and make a clear finger-to-eye signal, not only to those directly involved, but also to the rest of the players in the area. Speak, if you think it necessary, to calm nerves and add weight to your authority.

• Hold the restart signal until you are satisfied all is under control. There is no hurry. It if takes more than a few seconds, make an obvious gesture that you are stopping your watch, implying, "The game does not restart until you get your act together." Now, you are in charge.

• Remain visible. Pick a spot that gives you the best view of subsequent play and keeps you in eye contact with the players. If you are working with assistant referees on the diagonal system of control, be prepared to take an unusual position at a far-side corner kick. Istvan Zsolt, a famous Hungarian referee, caused a stir among colleagues when he moved off the diagonal, i.e., to the same side as the nearest assistant. When questioned, his reply was, "Sometimes I think it is more important for control that the players see me clearly in front of them. It depends on how I read the players' behavior. Occasionally, I use it as a surprise tactic. It works." Another effective ploy to emphasize your presence is to call out, "Watch it," "Take it easy," or a similar remark.

Too often in France '98, we saw attackers grabbed from behind, hugged like long-lost brothers, to block movement. We saw attackers rising to a high ball with elbows or arms flung into the defenders' faces. We saw shirts and shorts pulled to test fabric strength. We saw too much allowed to go unpunished because, in my opinion, referees did not control that phase of play before the restart. They were faced with multiple offenses from both teams and gave up.

If you follow the above plan and have to call an offense, you have given warning enough to stifle, or at least reduce, dissent. In addition, you may have avoided writing another discipline report.

Signals. Beware! Instinctive signals can be overdone. One referee drew negative comments for displaying mimed gestures for obvious restarts. He has the habit of going through the throw-in motion at practically every touch restart. Once or twice in a game, e.g., at close calls or disputed possession, that is good practice, but with an average of 35 throw-ins per game, the repeated gesture becomes pedantic and irritating. The same official whistled before goalkicks, with the same negative reaction.

Positively, the officials who used simple body language to mime offenses such as holding, backing into an opponent with arms outstretched, tripping with a scything movement, etc., earned good ratings for that aspect of control and communication. In some countries any attempts to communicate, other than by raising one arm to signify an indirect free kick, are frowned upon or actively discouraged. France '98 proved that attitude to be shortsighted in the best interests of the game. One contrived signal involved offside violations. The referee

... most corner kick tactics can be snuffed before they get out of hand at any level of soccer.

raised one arm to indicate an indirect free kick and passed the other across his body like a clock pendulum. For the same offense, another official pointed to his assistant and then toward the offending player. Both signals are unofficial, but both were attempts at communicating.

Avoid unnecessary gestures, keep mimes simple and relevant and press for a uniform code to help with the more difficult offenses.

Dissent. Excellent television coverage, with multiple views and angles, close-up action and professional editing gave us many opportunities to study the play for match control learning points. In general, the referees' decisions were confirmed in playbacks, often in slow motion, thus reducing confusion and, sometimes, critical interpretation by the commentators.

Unfortunately, the close-up shots also showed the constant dissent and abuse directed toward match officials who seemed powerless to handle it. The same criticism applies to officials at previous World Cup tournaments. Just as the tackle from behind became ingrained in soccer for many years, before it was seen as a serious threat to skill levels, we face a growing threat to the basic code of discipline necessary to keep the game attractive as a family sport.

To deal with dissent effectively requires a declaration of low tolerance to any act of indiscipline, backed by severe sanctions. Of the 258 yellow cards produced at France '98, only a few were given for dissent. One referee demonstrated a low-tolerance approach and was respected by the players for it.

Javier Castrilli of Argentina was that official, earning high ratings in his two matches. From the first whistle, Castrilli stamped on any form of dissent. He confronted the early offenders and, by clear body language, facial expression and verbal delivery, gave warning of his low-tolerance policy. In his second match, two players attempted to test him and were yellow carded.

> **To deal with dissent effectively requires a declaration of low tolerance to any act of indiscipline, backed by severe sanctions.**

Delay at restarts. At least five yellow cards appeared to caution players delaying restarts. One, for the Danish goalkeeper Schmeichel, was clearly merited because Schmeichel ignored the referee's repeated instruction to put the ball into play from a goalkick. Another, for delay while taking a free kick, was unjust. The player requested the 10 yards, the referee moved the defenders back except for one remaining about six yards from the ball. The referee whistled the restart but the kicker waited for the opponent to retire. He didn't and the referee became impatient, so out came the yellow card — for the kicker.

There was a similar incident at a corner kick. The kicker waited while an opponent stood five yards from the ball, the referee whistled, the kicker pointed to the opponent making no effort to retire and out came the yellow — again for the kicker. Those cautions might have been avoided had the officials used a simple technique: delay the restart until everyone is properly positioned.

The game is stopped; the ball is going nowhere until you give the say-so. Use the moment to impose control, just as was suggested when dealing with corner kick aggravation. Move to a position visible to all, make eye contact with the offending player, point to your watch or make a clear "stopping-watch" movement. Your message is, "You are gaining no advantage; move." It's an effective warning in most cases, for you put the onus on the player to act correctly. If not, no one is surprised if the yellow card appears.

A Players' Code

For more than 100 years, soccer has suffered from indiscipline and lack of knowledge of the basic rules as demonstrated in nearly every match by the principal actors and spectators. The toll of indiscipline at the World Cup — 258 cautions and 22 dismissals — tells its own story of the sorry state of the professional game and its example to youth and amateur players. Who can blame the latter when they behave as their idols? More disturbing is the climate of hate and aggression, manifested in the media and in the stands, in which officials are expected to control a match. What can be done to help the sport help itself?

We need a fresh approach to convince the whole soccer family that players and referees can work together for greater enjoyment of their favorite sport. The first big step is to motivate players to understand the *Laws of the Game*. As a player, I was never required, nor encouraged, to look at the rulebook. The clubs I played for required me to understand the rules of conduct within the club, but not on the field, the focal point of all members. I would have welcomed advice on the laws and been willing to take a test to prove my understanding of the discipline of

Referees, clubs and players would combine in a common interest to improve discipline on the field.

the game. After all, many activities require some degree of qualification, e.g., in motoring a learner must know the highway code before the practical driving test. Our school exams prepared us for practical life so, why not in sport? In soccer, it could be a players' code, a test on the basics of the laws and discipline.

How would it work? The test could be set for different levels of competition, e.g., schools, youth, amateur and professional. FIFA would be the leading authority to set a world standard. Competitions

would require clubs to include evidence of a players' code qualification along with other registration criteria.

Who would teach the players? That is where the referees come in, engaging the existing army of willing instructors to visit clubs and supervise the tests. Referees, clubs and players would combine in a common interest to improve discipline on the field. It could even help recruitment of match officials and reduce the annual loss of good servants through discontent. Players will become motivated to obtain a players' code certificate if the alternative is to not play. The certificate could also be a useful factor when dealing with discipline cases. Erring players could be required to retake the test and pass before playing again.

A players' code could be a vital factor to the future welfare of soccer, changing attitudes in a positive direction to reverse the trend of indiscipline endured for so long.

Thirty Years On: What's Changed?

Thirty years make one grain of sand in the history of the universe, but a near 20 percent mountain of soccer's existence as a modern sport. Against a backdrop of global suffering through wars, famine, violence and natural disasters, soccer continues to seduce millions with its charms as a stabilizing factor in a turbulent world. It's still the same old game: played with a round ball, chased by two teams on a rectangular field; same basic rules applied by a single official in the middle, bearing the frustrations of players and fans.

So, what has changed in the last three decades? In one word — attitude. Attitudes of players, coaches, fans and administrators have hardened. To win at all costs is now the norm, relegating the fun of playing and watching to secondary interest. Why? Again in one word — money.

At summit level, i.e., top professional leagues and international, the game is awash with the stuff. Soccer is big-time showbiz, a great vehicle for marketeers to sell their wares. The sport has always attracted media attention, but the boom of media cash cannons has become deafening within the last few years. Irresistible. The effect has been to impose enormous demands on the principal actors to get results.

Where has that gotten the match official? Way behind. The referee, the least considered and most abused component in the soccer equation, has been loaded with a heavier burden — of responsibility — to impose the correct conduct of play. In the spotlight of television scrutiny, errors or inefficiencies are magnified beyond the tradition of sporting acceptance. How has the referee coped with that demand to make the right call?

Match control studies of World Cup tournaments going back to 1966 produced the following conclusions: "Very little progress has been accomplished in resolving problems of match control identified 28 years ago."

Lack of help for referees was expressed in a cry from the heart of an international referee with experience of two recent World Cups, who said, "We need help, training, support, guidance, coaching, encouragement, etc." With the right priority allocated to improving match control, and given that 100 percent efficiency is unrealistic, an average of 95 percent should be the target at top-level.

The sport has always attracted media attention, but the boom of media cash cannons has become deafening within the last few years.

Suggestions to FIFA included a conference of FIFA referee instructors to coordinate instruction policy worldwide (proposed 1971); an International Refereeing Academy (1982); a FIFA-contracted panel of professional referees for international duties (1994).

The Refereeing Academy was set up in 1983 but shelved due to lack of sponsorship. However, following the election of Joseph S. Blatter as president (1998) and ex-international referee Michel Zen-Ruffinen as general secretary, FIFA staged the first world instructors' conference in Munich in February 2000.

Also announced in November 1999, was the formation of a group of pro referees under contract to FIFA and a group of full-time instructors. Good news, at last!

Rules 1976-2001. Modern technology's influences on soccer equipment; efforts to combat rules abuses and cheating; more responsibility for referees and assistants; a sacred principle abandoned; a 100-year-old rule scrapped and a rewrite of the *Laws* *of the Game* are the main items changed by the International Football Association Board.

Equipment and footwear (law 4). The 1975 rule carried nearly 300 words to limit the danger of cleats and bars on footwear, more to guide manufacturers than officials. Today, footwear is just one word in the list of compulsory equipment with overall responsibility put on the player "not to wear anything which is dangerous to himself or another player."

Abuses and cheating (law 12). Referees are sometimes the cause of law changes by not applying the letter so that abuses become accepted as "current practice." The classic example: goalkeeper possession judged by the number of steps while holding the ball.

In 1931, the limit of two steps changed to four for the reason that goalkeepers invariably infringed the law by taking three or more steps."

Over the years, referees let that practice get out of hand. Four steps became six, eight, 10, until Dino Zoff, Italy's goalkeeper, openly flouted the rule in World Cup games by taking as many as 12 steps. In February 2000, the IFAB accepted defeat by scrapping the 100-year-old step rule in favor of a time limit of six seconds.

For 30 years, the tackle from behind has destroyed much skill. Attempts to eliminate, by rule, have been partially successful, but it is still a problem.

Goalkeepers won another reprieve at penalty kicks when the 1929 rule restricting movement along the goalline, ignored by most referees, was abandoned in 1997. Although advancing from the goalline toward the ball is illegal, abuses are becoming current practice.

Boring defensive tactics led to the exclusion of handling the ball when received from a teammate, as a deliberate pass from the foot or throw-in (1992 and 1997, respectively). A good move that has opened up play.

For 30 years, the tackle from behind has destroyed much skill. Attempts to eliminate, by rule, have been partially successful, but it is still a problem.

Two important changes, aimed at cheating, require sending off players who deny an obvious goal-scoring opportunity and a caution for acts intended to deceive referees.

Coaches. Soccer coaches became legitimate in 1993, setting aside a 130-year sacred principle that the players play without outside help or interference. The coaches face two conditions: they must give instructions from a specified place and act in a responsible manner. But those are respected more in the breach than in the observance, like the four-step rule. Thus, there are more duties and aggravation for the officials! So, what's new?

Laws of the Game **rewrite.** A long overdue attempt to simplify the rulebook, overloaded with repetition and non-essentials, left us with a skeleton guide that requires much interpretation for practical application. That means more work for instructors and a greater need for publications that inform, advise and encourage further study.

The "Hand of God"

On any day, Azteca Stadium in Mexico City is an awe-inspiring sight — an oasis of luscious green on the floor of a vast arena. Huge banks of terraces angle up and away to the sky and, while the lower third is open to the heavens, the upper tiers are topped with a curving roof, cantilevered to provide all with a clear view of the action and a sound cavern that collects and throws the roars of the crowd down to the field.

At high noon on June 22, 1986, 114,580 fans packed the stadium for the World Cup quarterfinal match between bitter rivals Argentina and England. Little did anyone suspect that a few minutes into the second period, a routine flip back to the English goalkeeper from a teammate would lead to perhaps the most controversial goal in soccer history.

Bitter memories of the 1982 Falklands War still smoldered between the two nations, and the unsavory 1966 World Cup encounter between the two teams at Wembley Stadium led to the birth of the red and yellow card system. All was set for an exciting and competitive game.

Argentina, which would eventually beat West Germany in the final, headed its qualifying group and put out Uruguay, 1-0, in the previous round, while England just scraped through in second place on a goal difference before thumping Paraguay, 3-0, for the privilege of meeting Argentina in the quarterfinal match.

Commenting on the performances of referees in the first and second rounds, then-FIFA President Joao Havelange rebuked the officials for a too-lenient attitude, calling for strict compliance with FIFA directives and more efficient service when running the touchlines.

Not surprisingly the choice of referee for the Argentina-England clash aroused special interest. FIFA underlined the growing status of third world officials by selecting Ali Bennaceur of Tunisia as referee, together with Costa Rican Berny Ulloa Morera and Bogdan Dotschev from Bulgaria as linesmen.

The two teams tried to prepare quietly but an intense media build-up promised a match of fire and brimstone.

Bennaceur had performed well in his first-round assignment — a Poland-Portugal tie — and was confident. "I felt I had the full support of the referees' committee and my colleagues," said Bennaceur. "Apart from the president's call for tighter control, I also had a quiet word of advice from my friend, (then-referee's committee member) 'Tiny' Wharton, who reminded me to judge only what I saw and to resist any attempts to influence my decisions."

Of his linesmen Ali said, "Although we had no common language — Berny spoke only Spanish and Bogdan, Bulgarian — interpreters were available. I'd already (worked with) Bogdan in the Paraguay versus Belgium match. Berny was excellent and was even selected later to line in the final."

The two teams tried to prepare quietly but an intense media build-up promised a match of fire and brimstone. Argentina wore traditional blue and white shirts, black shorts and white socks; England was in white shirts, light blue shorts and white socks.

Diego Maradona, Argentina's captain, had already stamped his genius on the tournament and was the man to stop. However, England's Steve Hodge said, "We made no special plans to mark him tight. Later we realized we'd made a mistake."

As the contest unfolded, the play didn't match the splendor of the occasion. A scoreless first half was a dull affair of cautious spoiling tactics. England conceded midfield territory, smothering sporadic raids outside its penalty area. Argentina, fearing the talents of strikers Lineker and Beardsley, decided on close marking tactics, leaving the English little support to create chances. It was completely forgettable.

Six minutes into the second period, things were still dull. And then Maradona scored! But how? The crowd perked up at that change in the action.

Hodge describes his part: "I decided to flick the ball back to (goalkeeper Peter Shilton). I saw Maradona run at Peter, but not seeing any danger, I turned away. Then," Hodge added, "I heard a roar. The ball was in the net — I thought Maradona had headed it in."

English players chased Bennaceur to the center circle, tapping their hands to indicate a handling offense. Bennaceur eye-checked with linesman Dotschev, who was now running to the halfway line to take position for the restart. No problem. Bennaceur waved the protesting players away and got on with the game, 1-0.

Afterward, TV replays and photos from various angles proved the illegality of Maradona's first goal, ...

Four minutes later Maradona again scored. Gathering the ball in his own half, he charged forward, accelerating away from Hodge, past opponent after opponent. He rode a weak tackle from one English player and calmly side-tapped the ball into Shilton's net. Pure soccer genius! It is still considered one of the finest scoring runs in the annals of the World Cup. Argentina now led, 2-0.

England soon struck back. Lineker headed in a goal from a left wing cross to produce a dramatic last 10 minutes, 2-1. With two minutes remaining, the English again put the ball across but

Lineker's header shaved the wrong side of the goalpost. England had left it too late to attack and paid the price — elimination.

Afterward, TV replays and photos from various angles proved the illegality of Maradona's first goal, turning a critical spotlight on Bennaceur and Dotschev. "How did they miss it?" ran the sports pages. "Replay the match!" they demanded.

Bennaceur, now head of Tunisian referees, has only one regret: "I refereed at the international level for 17 years with much success, but people only remember me for that one incident. Incidentally, I received a high mark from FIFA for my handling of the match," he adds with a chuckle.

Confronted, Maradona said the first goal was scored "partly by the hand of God and partly by the head of Maradona."

Global indignation and cries of cheating drew a cynical postscript from English player Peter Reid. "If one of our lads had done it," he said, "I'd have said, 'Great, son!'"

Bibliography

The following are a few excellent publications worth a place in your soccer library.

Soccer Officials Guidebook, by Carl P. Schwartz, *Referee* Enterprises Inc. Franksville, Wis. 53126

Soccer Talk, by Paul Gardner, Masterpress, Lincolnwood, Ill. 60646

For the Good of the Game, Robert Evans and Edward Bellion, Youth Sports Publishing, Chatsworth, Calif. 91311

In Search of Fair Play, by D.C. Emerson Mathurin, ONEREAL, Ontario, Canada K1C 6J5

The Inner Game of Soccer, by Eric Sellin, World Publications, Mountain View. Calif. 94040

Fair or Foul, by Paul and Larry Harris, Soccer for Americans, Manhattan Beach. Calif. 90266

Official Soccer Rules Illustrated, by Stanley Lover, Triumph Books, Chicago, Ill. 60605

Soccer Rules Explained, by Stanley Lover, The Lyons Press/The Globe Pequot Press, Guilford, Conn. 06437

Thinking Soccer — Officiating Success Techniques, by Jeffrey Stern, *Referee* Enterprises Inc. Franksville, Wis. 53126

Smart Moves